THE
COLLEGE
SCENE

Students Tell It Like It Is

JAMES A. FOLEY
and
ROBERT K. FOLEY
Co-Directors of the College Poll

COWLES BOOK COMPANY, INC.
NEW YORK

To our family,
all of whom have had a hand
in this study

ACKNOWLEDGMENTS

These interviews, the tabulations, collation, and reports that follow were made possible by many persons. In particular, we wish to thank William J. Papp for his editorial direction; researchers Lila Murphy, Kathleen Shally, and Pat Perkins; interview coordinators, Pat Scanlan and Eileen Opfer; our statisticians, John Moore and Darrell Dewey; our sales consultant, Leyton Carter; and our editorial and broadcast associates, Joseph Boychuk, William Thomas, Robert Wogan, Robert Maurer, and Bill Ryan, of NBC *Monitor*.

We also wish to acknowledge the assistance of the Office of Education of the Department of Health, Education, and Welfare (HEW); the American Association of Colleges and Universities; the National Education Association; and the hundreds of college officials, faculty members, and student officers who have cooperated in this effort.

COLLEGE STUDENTS ADVISORY STAFF

Teresa Linskey	University of Connecticut
Cathleen Gast	Ladycliff College
Jock Willers	Bucknell University
Randy Bennett	Bradley University
Mark Beaugard	St. Louis University
Mark Willers	University of Southern California
David Kearney	University of Miami
Karen Singer	University of Oregon
Susan Rosenberry	University of Washington
Nicholas O'Connor	Notre Dame University
David McAuliffe	Boston College
Gail Anderson	Goucher College
Cynthia Honn	Wheaton College
Derek Carroll	Sante Fe University
Peter Marshall	Stanford University
Kent Beesinger	University of California, Berkeley
Melissa Ricci	Briarcliff College
Vincent Whiteig	St. Joseph's College
Kathleen Opher	Baldwin-Wallace College
Patricia Perkins	University of New Hampshire
Barbara White	Connecticut College for Women
Robert Sheehy	Bowdoin College
Marianne Foley	Marymount College
Steve Zimmerman	Columbia University
Louis Hipp	Duke University
Karen Fisher	Colorado College
David Carroll	Dartmouth College
Robert Brockway	New York University

PREFACE

Czar Nicholas of Russia is reported to have said after the Russian people revolted, "If I *really* knew how they felt about me, I would have acted quite differently."

Lack of communication ("dialogue" is the current "in" word) has caused wars, failures, and, even in the human terms, divorces and sadness.

The College Poll was created to establish a dialogue between the college generation, their parents, and elders as well as among themselves. Through thousands of personal interviews on more than a hundred campuses, with a cross section of the nation's college students, the College Poll has been refining student attitudes on virtually every subject of the day—political, economic, and social. Using established scientific polling techniques, the findings have been reduced to data-processed conclusions and editorial reports.

While many of the results of the College Poll have been released to the nation's leading newspapers and over NBC's *Monitor* (which has helped support the effort), this text is the first compilation of all the findings, including some new studies that have not yet been released.

The College Poll is a continuing study. We shall continue to report findings from year to year. Our international study, through our affiliates in eleven countries, is now under way. In this way, trend studies can be made, and a data bank on the college generation's thoughts and feelings on all manner of topics can be compiled.

We have tried to tell this story in the students' own words,

and have added background based upon our personal obser-
vations and those of our student interviewers, who have spent
hours and days sounding out students' own attitudes in dormitories, fraternity houses, and in just plain campus bull sessions in every section of the country.

We hope that parents and men and women of the older generation will, after reading this study, at least be aware of how
the college generation really feels. A great deal could be accomplished if students and parents knew that much alone.
For it is quite possible that the generation gap is a chasm that
can be closed with greater ease than either side imagines. It
starts with understanding.

The Authors

CONTENTS

THE
COLLEGE
SCENE

CHAPTER ONE

The Campus Scene

It is important from the very beginning to understand that it is as difficult to find the "average college student" as it is the "average man." The so-called college campus is a many-sided institution.

There are almost seven million full-time college students in the United States. This is more people than now live in Sweden. More than twice as many men and women go to college as there are people in the whole nations of Ireland or Israel. They are a very democratic group. They come from a cross section of American life and background. Not too many generations ago, the college student was largely a product of the privileged class—and a college education was the natural right of only a very limited segment of our society. As late as 1930, only 25 percent of the nation went from grammar school into high school. And the chances of a student moving on to college were 3 to 4 percent.

It was this elite group that lived in the dormitories, established the societies, shaped the traditions, and reaped the benefits of college and graduate school education. The entire college atmosphere, particularly in the resident schools, resembled that of a club for gentlemen and gentlewomen. There were, of course, exceptions, especially in the large urban and state schools where college degrees could be obtained on a lesser investment. Scholarships for needy but talented students were available on a limited basis in all schools. But on the whole, the concept of a college education for all has been of recent origin.

In a broad sense, education has become deified in this country. It started first at the high school level. Most parents of today's college students have enjoyed at least a high school education. On the other hand, most of the students' grandparents received nothing more than a grammar school education. The value and necessity of a college education were drummed into their minds and hearts since childhood.

"You'll never get a good job without a college education," or "I want you to go to college and be a success."

"Your mother and I are doing everything to send you to college; we want you to succeed."

These are typical expressions of the parents of the current generation, many of whom have seen their contemporaries succeed on the basis of a broader education. All too often, fathers have seen younger men climb to the top because, in their opinion, they have reaped the benefits of a college degree. In most parents' minds, a college education has become part of the necessary equipment for the attainment of material success. No sacrifice is too large, no demand too severe to provide their son with a college education—now at a price realistically beyond the means of most families.

The same has become true of daughters. Once, not too many generations ago, a college education was the luxury of wealthy girls, or schooling encouraged only for those with a career involving special training such as teaching and nursing. Today, however, the whole atmosphere has changed. Girls of varying backgrounds are in college preparing for either business careers or lifetime companionship with their equally educated husbands.

Veterans' benefits after World War II had a great effect, bringing higher education within the reach of millions and creating, in turn, an educated class. In most instances, this educated class rose to the top of their generation in material success, thus putting pressure on them to educate their own children.

The total result was an explosion of the college population. Federal and state governments appropriated vast sums to expand college facilities. Existing colleges and universities started vast expansion programs. New colleges were created. Junior colleges sprang up across the country. The explosion is still going on. The college population for 1970 is estimated to be ten million if present trends continue.

The college scene is no longer the ivy-lined Gothic campus personified in Hollywood movies of the 1940s, populated by a disciplined, socially oriented fraternity brother or coed. The college campus has become a variety of places. Michigan State's sprawling campus at East Lansing is a veritable city in itself. Here huge dormitories are self-contained communities, with recreation facilities that include swimming pools, libraries, cafeterias, clubs, and restaurants.

On the banks of the Hudson, girls in Bard College live in relaxed luxury. Students at Villanova, Ladycliff, and other schools may share rooms with three or four in older buildings long since overcrowded. At MIT, coeds live in a posh dormitory with wall-to-wall carpeting and antique furniture. At the University of Miami, students live in a tropically oriented modern campus at Coral Gables. And California students attend modern new colleges in beautiful Santa Barbara and similar cities along the magnificent California coastline.

A great many students do not reside on the campus at all. Off-campus living for students is a part of college life. Students who live off campus at Columbia and Harvard find themselves in university-owned converted tenements which are little more than cheap "rooming houses," as the Columbia report put it. Similar slumlike apartments house students at the University of Chicago, Johns Hopkins, the University of California, and Dayton. Yet at Washington State, off-campus living can signify a modern apartment house at costs far less than a family pays for similar facilities. Even at Harvard, the university has also erected a modern five-hundred family unit for married students along the Charles River. At NYU, the large educational complex that has taken over Washington Square, the university has lined that once grand park with modern, low-cost dormitories, and bought a housing development nearby for students and faculty.

It is also forgotten that a very large percentage of American college students do not live even near the campus, but reside at home. The "day hop" comprises almost 40 percent of the college population. They live at home, commute by car to and from the local college and have an entirely different feeling of "campus life" than the student who lives in the decaying fraternity houses on a sprawling campus like Ohio Wesleyan. In fact, one of the biggest problems facing all colleges is the ever-expanding "parking lot" that has eaten up campus space in suburban schools, and dormitory space in city colleges. To the day hop, the parking place is the number-one obstacle to his education.

The thousands who attend colleges like Jersey City's St. Peters, the downtown Chicago branch of Northwestern, or Marquette in Milwaukee have little in common with the Radcliffe junior who frolics in jeans and a convertible on the Massachusetts campus. Yet they are all part of the college generation, who today are being studied, analyzed, and, in large measure, condemned as a simple, easily identified entity.

Today's college generation, however, cannot easily be categorized demographically. With the base of college education broadening, the college student comes from an ever-widening segment of American society. Whereas twenty-five years ago, the college generation consisted of students whose parents had an annual income of $25,000 or more, today's students are able to attend college regardless of their family's income. The College Poll figures show that most students' families report incomes of $12,000. Student aid programs, scholarships, and loan funds have made a college education available to nearly any qualified student.

Today's college students come from the homes of union workers; black, Jewish, and Italian ghettos; palatial mansions in Grosse Pointe; drugstore owners; garage mechanics; bank presidents; and even relief recipients. Thus, they are forced into an atmosphere as democratic as American life itself—not the privileged, affluent class so often identified with the college generation.

In addition, they are more mature than members of previous college generations. Maturity is a relative term, it is true. But in age and mental capacity, the contemporary student arrives at the college age in a state of mental, physical, and social awareness far beyond his counterpart of generations past. Today's students are, indeed, masters of an intricate technology of physics, economic analysis, computers, and medical and psychological science that did not exist in their fathers' and mothers' generation. In truth, today's college freshman has a broader education than the college graduate of yesteryear.

A professor at Michigan State explained it well when he said, "The students of this generation have had to absorb more knowledge, file it away in order, recall it quickly on command, and apply it in a variety of situations never conceived by previous generations."

Students of the sixties have reaped the benefits of being exposed to a communications explosion—the result of the electronic miracles of our era. They read, converse, and live on a scale and at a pace that are both different from and more personal than previous generations. The college student has been exposed to all the many aspects of life such as sex, money, divorce, Medicare, war, dishonesty, violence, and scandal on probably much more intimate terms than his father or mother. There may be reasons to question his wisdom, philosophy, and even his judgment. But his awareness of life in all its many forms makes him opinionated and less capable of naïveté. He is certainly less susceptible to non-factual persuasion and blind submission to decisions than his less experience-oriented elders.

Today's campus is unique in other ways as well. The college itself is an entirely different institution. Gone, probably forever, is the home away from home to which parents sent their sons and daughters to be educated under the benign but stern tutelage of educators, who watched out for the physical, mental, and moral progress of their young charges. The whole concept of *in loco parentis* is not only rejected by both student and college alike—it is a physical improbability. The Barnard College president who had to debate the supervision of her off-campus student, living openly off campus with an unmarried male student from nearby Columbia, pointed up the dilemma of the college administrator who has little effective control over the activities of his or her students.

Even if they still wanted this responsibility, and students would accept it, the college president and administration are a harassed and too-little appreciated factor in the college population explosion. In the tranquil era of education, decades past, orderly growth of the college was made possible by fund drives from alumni, or by a petition to the legislature in the case of state institutions. Presidents, hired more for their fund-raising abilities than for their educational qualifications, had little time for the curriculum reforms, faculty problems, and student orientation problems that plagued the college and university from other aspects.

The pressures on college presidents to raise funds, pacify trustees, orient doubting legislatures have, perforce, separated them from the mainstream of college life. The dean, who for years planned orderly courses with a fatherly tolerant eye on students, and an academic rapport with his faculty, has found himself confronted with demands for courses that are more relevant to a generation he hardly understands. On the whole, he is trying sincerely and valiantly to keep a historical and professional attitude toward the flood of new areas that need to be covered by some academic discipline.

The faculty, which once enjoyed a tranquil and contemplative existence in most schools, has undergone a complete orientation. The scholar, who purveyed wisdom and inspiration to adoring students, is now a business-oriented professional harassed by his own difficulties with both the institution and the student body. Pressed to continue his professional education, subjected to doubts as to the validity of his contribution to the university and his own future, the college professor today is an entirely different breed from his predecessor. All too often he has lost both the confidence of his students and the rapport with his deans and administrators. While his personal economic plight has been improved in recent years by increased salary and outside employment, the faculty member today is subjected to the same impersonal atmosphere and rigid moral pressures that plague the whole college campus.

It is tragic that violence has arrived on the campus. The process of change had too little chance of successful achievement without the added impediment of violence. Change had to come, of course. The adult student of today could hardly accept many of the limitations placed upon his personal life and mental stimulation that were the result of an archaic design of the curriculum—a design meant for a different age and time.

The harassed administration, trying to establish priorities, was not prepared to cope with the insistence of the student's demands or the immediacy of his needs. Certainly the college administrators are not politicians, able to manipulate political and social demands adroitly. They were never intended to be. Nor are faculty members, trained in a specific discipline, suitable arbitrators in areas in which they have the same doubts and suspicions that badger the students.

This generation has no illusions as to the hierarchy of the college educated. While their parents may be proud in the reflected glory of the baccalaureate in the family, the college student himself does not expect the college education to have the immediate or long-term values that parents expect of the degree. The college degree is no longer the badge of the social or educated elite—but an economic necessity.

The cross section of student opinion reflects a growing disbelief that a college education leads either to fulfillment or satisfaction. While a larger segment of career-oriented students, motivated to pursue engineering, law, medicine, or other definite programs, is less concerned about basic attitudes, even they reflect the doubts most students feel about the university life and its goals.

Students find the impersonal nature of life in general reflected in their college environment. Studies are designed for specialization, and supply no real personal meaning to the existence of a mature and dedicated undergraduate. Schools become vocational factories; and courses, perhaps because of an antiquated and often irrelevant curriculum— which many regard as superficial and unrelated to life— prepare man to fulfill a limited and narrowly channeled role in a mechanized life where success is measured in material terms, and life degenerates into a suburban bore or urban rot.

Aware of the social and economic ills of the day, students of all backgrounds question their place and function in the future. With an unpopular war hovering over their heads, students wonder why they must spend four of the most vital, vibrant, and productive years of their lives studying subjects that provide no answers to these problems. Professors with their overloaded work programs have little time for questions or dialogue. Students who are not ready to specialize gravitate toward a limbo area of knowledge officials consider to be unscholarly. Adult in mind, body, and the depth of their emotions, they regard as unworkable and ridiculous the rules of yesteryear that tend to restrict their opportunities for personal decision-making.

Trained to question, they properly ask the meaning of much that surrounds them. All too often parents have no ready answers and even resent the questions put to them by their inquiring offspring. The school, busy with economic survival, has little time. Many faculty members have little understanding or interest. As a result, frustrations build, and the fuse burns shorter.

Generally speaking, all parties—students, faculty, and administrators alike—have agreed in good faith that change is necessary and desirable. Most of all, there is a need for patience, tolerance, and understanding on all sides. Extremists have been eloquent in the presentation of their cases. The racial student and repressive administration have found a ready press. It is to be questioned whether the instant dissemination of events by our communication media has been helpful or harmful in presenting the case for either faction. The student is not always wrong in requesting change, nor is the administration always at fault in resisting it. If both sides are not to be polarized into prolonged confrontation, and reasonable compromises achieved, a basic broad dialogue with all students must be established.

To this end, the College Poll was formed, to reflect the attitudes of a cross section of all students by means of in-depth interviews with students, using professional techniques and scientific sampling methods. The College Poll was started at the request of a group of newspaper editors who felt the need of a more representative expression of the attitudes of the college generation. While the primary requisite was for a balanced news source from the campus, the interviews provide, in their coverage of a broad spectrum of subjects, a clear reflection of the thinking of students about the social, economic, and political issues of the day. More important, it was hoped that the results of the poll would provide a clear insight into the reasons for student beliefs.

To faculty, administrations, and legislatures alike, who would deal with this problem of change in our university life, these student attitudes may be revealing and helpful. Parents who encountered difficulty in trying to communicate with their college-age offspring may find, at least, the basis for the difference in attitudes—if not a complete solution to the inadequacy of expression that so plagues the parental relationship today, on both sides. For students themselves, this delineation of a broad segment of undergraduate opinion may supply the stimulation for a more moderate and constructive voice in campus affairs that would bring some order out of chaos and progress out of pain.

The college generation must not and cannot be ignored. Properly channeled, the efforts for good of America's young men and women can be substantial. They bring to the world ideals and a sense of dedication few generations have offered to their particular periods in time. Ignored, they have produced a tumult of violence that is having an increasingly dangerous impact on education and the institutions designed to provide that education.

Their success in bringing reform through action has evidently made an impression on the new classes graduating from high schools. The example of foment on the college campus is now extending to the high school students. They are the college students of the next four years and even beyond.

Those who think repression will be the answer labor under a grave misunderstanding as to the determination and depth of student convictions. Stricter laws, financial sanctions, and giving college officials discretion and less authority to deal with problems will, in the opinion of many experts, prolong the dissent and accelerate the confrontation. While students almost unanimously believe in law observance, they almost equally agree that the use of force, moral or physical on either side, will increase tensions. Rational solutions, or at least a willingness to seek common-sense accommodations must be forthcoming from the administration and faculty sector if laws are to be observed.

If we are not to face an era of confrontation, steps must be found to establish and continue the dialogue. The college student has much to say. Much frustration and pain can be avoided if he merely knows his audience is disposed to listen.

CHAPTER TWO

Black Students–
A New Campus Era Opens

It is ironic and paradoxical that the civil rights movement has made more progress on America's campuses than in any other segment of our society.

There is among American college students a deep and sincere sympathy for the black people. Also, university administrations, on the whole, have met blacks' problems with compassion and consideration. Given time and forbearance on both sides, the black's needs, if not his demands, might have been solved on the university level.

It may now be too late. Certainly, it is regrettable that, in an area where more than any other the gaps might have been bridged, we have growing separation and disheartening insurgency. In addition, the slow erosion of goodwill and the hardening of positions on both sides will make solutions more difficult to achieve.

A review of the background of the black student on campus would probably be helpful, for his problem is different from any other—and solutions must be based on compromises that neither party seems able to make at present.

Interestingly enough, the College Poll shows that most college students are not prejudiced against blacks on the campus. When students were asked the question last year, "How are Negroes treated on your campus?", 55 percent said, "No different from other students." Thirty-one percent said, "Slightly different."

Most white collegians had little contact with blacks but were quite happy to see them on the campus. Every effort was made to eliminate prejudice, especially in those areas where students themselves had control, e.g., fraternities, sororities, and student organizations. The College Poll interviews also revealed that whites took no active role in welcoming black students. The reason is that they felt blacks should be "treated like everyone else"—not singled out in any particular fashion.

As a matter of record, there really aren't many Negroes on American college campuses. Blacks total only slightly more than 250,000 among the nation's nearly seven-million full-time college population. Almost 30 percent of them are located at Negro colleges like Roosevelt, Grambling, and Lincoln. Only in the past five years has there been any real influx of black students to the general campus scene—in itself an indication of the education gap in the country.

The educational community has tried hard to remedy the situation, a fact that is overlooked by all sides amidst the current crisis. College administrations literally "rewrote the book," as one president put it, to get more blacks into schools. Committees were formed to encourage black students to go to college. Realizing that black people need higher education as a group, universities recruited likely black candidates in high schools, using tests and the recommendations of principals to select those who, regardless of income, might be able to make it in college. Hundreds of scholarships were set up. In those situations where blacks were obviously not ready to handle college work, arrangements were made to send them to topflight prep schools to help them get into college. Thus Choate, Loomis, Cromwell, and Exeter all had black students on full scholarship with an assurance of admission to Ivy League colleges—an assurance their white classmates did not have.

On a larger scale, college admission boards were directed to accept students from more diversified backgrounds, including an increasing percentage of Negroes. This year, for example, the Ivy League colleges reserved nearly one thousand admissions out of a total of eight thousand freshmen for Negroes. In the selection of women for Yale, great care was used to make sure that a proper percentage of Negroes was admitted. These percentages are even more impressive when one realizes that only the top 10 percent of all high school and prep school students are eligible for the Ivy League colleges. The same is true at Stanford (the Ivy League college of the West Coast) and other schools with high entrance requirements.

Both students and administrations are beginning to wonder if the experiment is successful. College officials are visibly shocked at the reaction of the Negroes to this open-door policy. As one dean put it:

"It's not that we expected gratitude from the black students, but we never expected a belligerent and aggressive policy to change the institutions to suit black demands."

The black student has, in general, been unimpressed with the efforts on the part of educators to provide higher education regardless of finances or background. Black student leaders have made it clear that they feel they are on the campus to "ease the social conscience" of the white establishment. Other black leaders have claimed that black students are being used to provide a "healthy picture," that they are being used as social guinea pigs.

It is just possible that the admissions experiment may have been premature. Blacks on the campus have found integration difficult, if not impossible. Despite the cooperation of white students, College Poll interviews show that blacks have found it difficult to be at ease or at home, particularly in the Ivy League type of college. The difference in background between the Negro and white student has become accentuated rather than reduced. As a small minority on the campus, Negroes have tended to stick together, not by enforced segregation, but by social preference. While there are exceptions on every campus, Negro eating tables have become evident. At social functions, Negroes customarily stick with their own group. This has been true in all cases where minorities appear on campuses.

"A Chinaman always seeks out another Chinaman" was the opinion of a student at San Francisco University when questioned about this phenomenon. "It's quite normal that Negroes would congregate."

Unfortunately, the resultant atmosphere of tension and unease has resulted in a polarization of the Negro among his black brothers and sisters. A black student at Princeton put it quite bluntly: "I've decided I don't like the white establishment. I don't want to be trained to take my place in a white society where I really don't belong. I have nothing against the men here at Princeton personally, but I'll never be eligible to really join in their world. If I am going to be of use as a black educated man and be of value to my black people, I am never going to get it here at Princeton the way it is."

The dissatisfaction is not only social. Black students have learned that the curriculum is not suitable to them. If they accept the principle that they want to be black instead of white, as more and more do, they object to studies that they feel are leading them into a white world where they'll never fit.

Of even greater concern to university administrators and faculty is the small hard-core group of Negroes who point with contempt and resentment to certain university activities as an indication of how the white establishment is oppressing the Negro in other areas. Negro leaders at Chicago University and at Northwestern, for example, have cited the universities' expansion into the surrounding Negro ghetto as an indication of callous disregard for the welfare of black people. To a lesser extent the same demand was made at Harvard and Columbia.

Out of this situation has arisen a sort of black solidarity the College Poll interviews reveal. Instead of integration, the "Negro" no longer exists. He now wants to be known as black. He wants black studies and black power. In their dress on the campus, more and more Negroes assume the Afro-American hair style. They are unimpressed with invitations to join white fraternities. In the spring of 1969 the black student body, as a student leader at Wayne stated, "found itself."

"It is not that we're antiwhite or antianything," said a Columbia black student. "We want our university to become meaningful to us. We want our education to be a black education. We want it to be real."

At first, the movement was peaceful. The black leaders had a positive approach. Afro-American society chapters were formed on most campuses where there were any appreciable number of negroes. Student leaders were appointed and, in general, a nonviolent approach to demands for change took place. With the exception of Columbia, where radical black leaders led the sit-in, most black students were willing to follow a course of nonviolent protest. The other key exception was at San Francisco State, which had overtones other than those of merely black power. Moreover, San Francisco State is a day school, closely tied in with local racial conditions and is not representative of the resident-black college attitude.

The first reaction from college administrations was tolerant and sympathetic. The Negro demands were at least consistent with their attitude toward education. In brief, they wanted Afro-American studies that gave to the black student pride in his heritage. At first the demand was to have special courses on their Negro heritage, both in Africa and in this country. Students pointed out logically that the Negro was left out of the white-oriented curriculum, a fact with which most college officials agreed. The charge was that the courses contained no references to Negroes, or the contribution they had made to civilization or history. Black heroes of all wars were ignored. Not only in history, but in literature, the arts, and sciences the role of blacks was eliminated— giving black students the feeling that only whites made the culture in which we live and work. Most college officials agreed. A deep study of the black's role and of black achievement was made, and integration of the black into courses is planned in most schools. It is not an easy accomplishment, requiring new texts and teaching aids. It takes time and money, but educational institutions agreed and the commitment was made.

It was not enough. Blacks soon found that "mere mention" is not sufficient. "They are still white courses for a white world." The demands were later intensified to include completely black integrated studies. College officials for the most part felt this was both unwise and impractical.

A professor of mathematics at the University of Chicago pointed out, "Algebra is algebra. It is no less algebra if we use examples of Negroes instead of whites in the problems."

Black students demanded courses in "problem-solving" in the ghetto areas; "the economics of poverty"; "money and banking" for the poor; and other similar programs that had direct relevancy to the ghetto areas. Such programs were impossible to put through on short notice. Yet administration and faculty groups made sincere efforts to try to meet black demands. Against the better judgment of many of their associates, faculties set up Afro-American courses in almost every major university and college in the United States. There was a shortage of books and materials, and of equal importance, professors to conduct these courses.

It was at this juncture that the second round of confrontations took place. Black students rejected white teachers as unqualified to instruct the black students in these courses.

"Whitey is prejudiced in what he says as well as what he reads" was the position of a UCLA black student.

Black students then demanded the right to approve and to appoint teachers to conduct Afro-American and similar courses. And it was at this stage during the early part of 1969 that black rapport with university officials began to deteriorate. Black courses are one thing. Even a black curriculum makes some sense. But control of the faculty was the prerogative of the university.

It probably all happened too fast. Black leaders obviously misinterpreted the original leniency of university administrative bodies and faculty senates. Encouraged to demand more by their early successes and backed by an increasingly militant attitude, the black students decided to "go for broke." The administrations were already battered by the militant arbitration demands of the S.D.S. rioters. Without a firm policy of their own and with faculties torn between a liberal and a conservative approach, the administrations in most cases vacillated. All too often they capitulated. It was at this stage that the militants took over.

The vulnerability of the university was never more evident than in the case of Cornell, which in many ways epitomized the situation throughout the country. In an attempt to avoid bloodshed, the administration made concessions and promises that were obviously insincere and rallied the moderate white students behind the blacks. Liberal professors fought with the conservative professors and the rift among the faculty was fortuitously exploited by the insurgents.

The Cornell administration and the faculty were divided in their opinions. In fact, it was questionable who could make a promise to the students that would be backed up with authority. The campus itself was torn between liberal attitudes toward the blacks and their objectives and the rejection of violence as a tool of accomplishing it. The appearance of guns—a logical but appalling extension of the violence— created an atmosphere of fear and, as one professor put it, "decisions were made at gun point." In any event the picture of Cornell black students leaving the buildings with guns has hurt the black cause everywhere.

Student reaction has been strong. This was not a case where insurgent police battered students into submission. The black movement became identified with violence itself and the liberal factions on campus found their sympathy toward the black movement changing to resentment. Consistent with their attitude against violence in all forms, most college students will not support black violence, especially when it is unprovoked and unchallenged.

The future is not optimistic. Black demands have increased rather than decreased. Black-student attitudes have consolidated behind their black leaders. Encouraged by the administrations' failure to act promptly and by their temporary success (which student leaders admit was far beyond expectations), black students intend to hold firm in 1969-1970.

Their demands may be irreconcilable. The vast majority of students will not support black demands for faculty approval and the right to hire and fire teachers for black courses.

When asked, "Should black students have the right to hire and fire teachers for black courses?", 68 percent of all students responded with an emphatic "No."

Nor will most students even back the full demands for black integrated courses. However, students do find some validity in Afro-American study plans in general.

When asked, "Do you believe there should be an Afro-American course at your school?", 78 percent of all students responded affirmatively.

But there is a difference of opinion as to whether or not it should be a degree course.

When asked, "Should Afro-American courses be offered as a major?", 42 percent said yes and 40 percent said no. The remaining students were undecided.

The concept of black students being educated for a black society is not consistent with most undergraduate ideas of civil rights or harmony between races. Students who fought the image of racism as being an expression of prejudice against blacks now fear that black racism is developing. Students are not sure it is in the best interests of both races to accentuate the difference.

"Afro-American courses are good for the school, but I think whites should take them," stated a Penn junior.

"We may be defeating the purpose of education if the black students study only 'soul courses' ", a Yale senior, told a College Poll interviewer.

Other students line up on the side of the black militants, as this statement by a CCNY white junior indicates:

"The black has been held back so long, we have to give him every break. If a black curriculum will help, that's what a university is for.

The lowering of admission standards, and similar black demands, is another area in which students do not hesitate to express themselves. For example, the College Poll interviewers learned that most students rejected the plan proposed by CCNY blacks and Puerto Ricans to permit admission by minorities to schools without qualifying examinations.

The average student's attitude in this respect, however, must be balanced against the whole area of college admissions. Most young men and women worked extremely hard to get into college. Passing the College Board examinations—a filtering point for college entrance—has been a major effort for every high school student. A mere passing grade is actually not enough. The higher the Board marks, the better chance the student has of gaining entrance to the college of his choice. Most Harvard and Yale students averaged 650-700 on their boards. Students who averaged in the neighborhood of 550 find themselves in colleges of lesser prestige—even though they may be very satisfactory for the student's own aptitude. But college entrance in almost every case has to be earned through an exhaustive and competitive series of tests.

Most students realize that many black students have difficulty with the College Boards. This difficulty arises from inadequate high school training and education. College students do not believe that blacks have any lesser intellectual potential than whites, but they do agree in most instances, that educational standards for blacks have been lower. And it must be admitted that white collegians have joined in the effort to open the door to more Negro opportunities, including scholarship grants, extra teaching, and even special consideration of college admission standards, provided the student has real potential.

"Not everyone is entitled to a college education because he is black," declared a Maryland sociology major, when questioned on this specific point. "But a college education should be available to anyone who is qualified, black or white."

"If we start giving away degrees, our college education won't mean anything," was the answer given by a Syracuse senior.

"Black students feel that any sheepskin will make them educated," said a Georgetown sophomore. "It's the education, not the sheepskin, that counts."

"Nobody becomes an educated man through soul studies," commented an NYU black student who is studying for a law degree. "Too many blacks are being deluded into thinking there can be a black and white society. We fought for integration and we are finding it harder the closer we get to it. It's no solution to start a separate educational process."

This student, typical of the dedicated, conservative black on campus, rejects most of the black movements. Those blacks who are from middle-class families, and particularly those who have come to campuses by means of their own hard work, having passed the College Boards, are against the Afro-American movement generally, the College Poll interviews show. However, they have lost control of the black campus movement, which is now firmly in the hands of the activists.

Separate courses, separate curricula, and black teachers are only part of the demands. Black students on some campuses now want black student-union buildings, dormitories, and recreation facilities. In these demands, they run afoul of the very antisegregation laws that were enacted to prevent discrimination against blacks. At Antioch College, the separate facilities for blacks had to be altered after the government threatened to halt aid because of civil rights law violations. Many professors and college authorities point out that some black demands may even be unconstitutional.

Black militants also are losing the backing of even the liberal faculty on these issues. There is much to be said on both sides. The demands of the Negro have raised basic doubts as to the function of the university. Trustees and administrations of all universities have begun to inquire whether or not a university should properly be used for political reasons. Even liberal college presidents have been forced to reevaluate their attitudes toward new courses and curricula in the face of increasing confrontations and demands. Scholars question the advisability of hastily conceived curricula.

Administration officials, hard pressed to make ends meet, question the economic outlay in setting up courses and departments geared to a small minority on the campus. The lack of qualified teachers and a bona fide curriculum has led to the establishment of an institute at NYU to study the means and methods of setting up proper educational guidelines for Afro-American studies.

Moreover, even if objectives are bona fide and valid, the timetable demanded by black students appears to many college officials too short for effective action.

Rather than rest on their laurels, black students have been increasing the tempo of their demands and the aggressiveness of their tactics. They demand complete amnesty for militants who run afoul of university regulations, yet continue to make plans for even greater aggression in the months ahead. What is pictured by most blacks is a whole new concept of the university with separate facilities and an even easier admission policy, separate grading standards, and separate courses, all black oriented. This objective will never get campus backing, in the opinion of students queried by the College Poll.

What also concerns students is the increasing belligerence of the black student organizations as their role has rapidly changed from a passive to an active one.

There appears to be a growing commitment to use force and violence on the part of black leaders.

"We must use apolitical means," said a Black Panther member to a group at a Columbia meeting. "Political means won't work. We've seen that. By apolitical we mean demonstrations, confrontations, and, if necessary, force."

This prospect is of deep concern to moderate campus leaders.

There is also a tendency to show solidarity in strength in campus functions. For example, at a recent lecture on black affairs at Penn State, the Afro-American students attended in a body—sitting in the balcony.

"We just wanted the campus to know we're not forgetting that's where we used to sit—and that we're all together on this issue," said an Afro-American leader.

Meanwhile, at Northwestern black students now congregate at "The Black House" on campus.

Of equal concern to university officials is the extreme right-wing campus group that has joined forces against the S.D.S. maneuvers. These groups are openly against further "concessions" to blacks or "pampering," as the Cornell conservatives have charged.

The atmosphere around campuses is tense on the black problem. News media seem disposed to give to black demon-

strations the same coverage they have afforded the radical
S.D.S. movement. Black leaders find the photographers, reporters, and television cameras ready to present their arguments freely—giving the movement a certain status that is
really out of proportion to the exigencies of the situation.
But the civil rights issue is always news, and black leaders
appear to have learned how to get press coverage from the
radical campus leaders.

On the whole, however, the blacks have kept apart from
the S.D.S. militants who are always willing to line up behind
black demands. In fact, the College Poll interviewers discovered in their rounds of American campuses that the blacks
do not seek the support of the S.D.S.

"The S.D.S. isn't a black movement. They are after many
things," commented a Columbia black leader when asked
about the white militant group. "We're only after one thing—
a black society on this campus. We wish they'd stay out of
our fight. They are trying to co-opt our struggle for white
ends."

The resentments that are building up come from a questioning of motives as well. In the school newspapers much
space is devoted to black problems. In interviews with black
campus leaders, students are told, "We are here to ease the
white conscience—to gloss over the years of slavery and
repression."

"We are symbols of the white sins, and you can't buy away
your guilt by giving us a white education, and trying to fit
us into white culture. We reject that. We reject white culture," a Negro Berkeley junior said with some heat to a
College Poll rep.

The backlash against the black cause spreads beyond the
campus. University officials and student organizations alike
fear enactment of legislation that would harden positions on
all elements of change on the campus.

Many universities are subject to state control and trustees
and administration officials are accountable to legislatures

for their funds. Restrictive legislation may well tie the hands of administration officials in helping to effect reasonable compromises on the campus. In the face of this, the black cause is sure to be hindered. In addition, in the coming years, black students are likely to be admitted to colleges from high school under a still more favorable admission policy and, in many cases, with full scholarship support. They will arrive on the campuses with an even more militant attitude, if the high school scene is any criterion.

The tragedy is that black students may have lost the goodwill of their classmates and may find a repressive and belligerent atmosphere in the years ahead. The even greater tragedy is that they represent less than 3 percent of the total campus population. The millions of other students who are dedicated to a traditional education and who have had sympathy for black students to date may find in the violence that is sure to result an irritating interruption in their own education. This, in turn, may create bitterness and resentment that will last for years to come.

Meeting the demands of the black students on the campus in the coming years will require common sense, compromise, and goodwill on both sides. It will also require restraint on the part of the press, radio, and television, and understanding by the public.

CHAPTER THREE

Student Views on Vietnam and the Draft

Mayor Richard Daley of Chicago blamed the confrontation between the police and students at the Democratic Convention largely on the Vietnam War. Many college presidents have indicated they believe the Vietnam War is responsible for much of the uproar on the campus. In large measure, they are correct.

The college student reflects the frustration of society as a whole toward the Vietnam War. Whereas the average American limits his objections to the war to writing letters to his congressman or to the editor of his local newspaper or voting for a new president, the college student tries to make his voice heard in some more articulate way. Moreover Vietnam is the war of the college generation. Most people have little contact with the war, except when a member of the family is in the service. But the Vietnam War is an ever-present reality to college students. It complicates their lives in ways little understood by the adult generation.

"Passing becomes almost a matter of life and death," explained a Northwestern sophomore. "It's hard to study well, take the right courses, or even develop a relationship with a prof when you both know if you flunk—you're in Vietnam."

"My roommate flunked out last year because he had a fight with a teacher," said an NYU junior. "Today he's in

Vietnam. The teacher was wrong and lousy at that. But that's what can happen."

"Our whole lives would change if the war was over," said a Bard college junior.

"You can't plan anything until this war is over," stated a Briarcliff junior.

A Goucher senior explained, "It's easy to say every generation had a war. But it's different this time because it's a limited fight. Men don't feel they are saving their country, although they are willing to do their duty. This war isn't really related to our lives, yet it affect's men's attitudes toward school, girls, and the future."

A California dean added, "To most of the population this is not a war generation—and students sense and resent this. Many of the frustrations and resentments against the war are manifest in demonstrations that would, in part, end with peace in Vietnam. Of course, there are forces for change in the college life that have little to do with the war, but some of the violence and confrontation would cease with the war's end."

There is another area that concerns students. Much of the money being used to fight the war is being diverted from urgent social programs in the United States. The cutback in urban programs, antipoverty funds, Head Start, and other social programs is, to students, another cost of the war. The arrival of peace, however, would free vast sums for these areas. College students want to concentrate more of the nation's resources on the solving of the social and economic ills of society, which they consider to be the root cause of much of the unrest in the nation.

The average college student doesn't understand the Vietnam War. Not that students are uninformed about Vietnam and its current history. In general, however, our Washington administrations have not convinced the college generation that entering the war was intelligent in the first place, nor that it has been handled well after we entered.

Undergraduates take particular issue with parents and their elders in the matter of reaction to news and propaganda. They believe that parents are too often prone to accept government statements and diplomatic policy blindly and without questioning the basic underlying facts upon which those policies are made. They question, also, our nation's honesty and integrity in announcing the reasons that we take certain actions in the world community. Campus opinion, for example, is that our government overthrew the Diem regime in Vietnam. They believe we have been instrumental or permissive in setting up or abandoning the various regimes that have since replaced the Diem government.

Students are armed with facts to support these beliefs and find that their elders are unacquainted with the details of the war's progress. Yet when students assert that we have handled various governments in a cavalier manner, they are often rebuffed with the argument that such talk is "unpatriotic" or "disloyal." The Vietnam War has served to point out to the younger generation that the American people know little about the underlying events that so concern their futures. Students of all economic levels report they have no dialogue in discussing with their parents the merits of either the war or the diplomatic maneuvers simply because parental decisions are largely emotional.

They refuse to accept decisions about which many members of the government are in complete disagreement, merely on the basis of being patriotic or "going along with your government." The whole area of the Tonkin Gulf decision, the use of Cambodia and Laos, the commitments and reassurances given the various governments is basically unknown to most adults but well understood and often debated by students. Disagreements about the cause of the war are one of the prime factors giving life and substance to the so-called generation gap, since these are issues in which emotions run high.

Students do not feel it is unpatriotic to question government ploys or decisions. Trained to be inquisitive, educated to be critical and objective, they feel that in applying these attributes to the issues of the day, they are carrying on a democratic tradition in keeping with the long-standing traditions of American democracy.

Frequently they do not consider Hanoi communistic in the same sense they consider Red China and Russia communistic. Both conservative and liberal students believe that the Vietnamese have a right to self-determination and if that means going communistic, it is a decision that must reside in the will of the Vietnamese people.

As for the war itself, the collegiate population is appalled by the slaughter of Vietnamese civilians by American troops. Conversations on campuses center upon the desolation of villages by napalm and the leveling of landscapes by bombs and heavy American artillery. It is, indeed, a paradox that students are not nearly so conscious or articulate about the very real atrocities carried on by the Viet Cong. Nor are they impressed by the terror tactics used by the Viet Cong during the last elections. The reason for this can be found in the general belief that much of this Viet Cong activity is caused by the presence of American troops. They seem to be reasonably well convinced that, if we pull out, the country would return to a normal way of life. And they are deeply resentful of any attempt by the United States to impose our democratic way of life on any country.

It is also quite obvious that students are adversely affected by the constant television coverage of the war, the scenes of children and elderly people being killed, and the graphic descriptions of defloration of the countryside.

In a purely political sense, they can't visualize Vietnam as a threat to our security. For the most part they do not regard Vietnam as a key element in the power play to contain Red China on the Asiatic continent. And even conceding that the students' view of these points may be provincial, their biggest uproar was precipitated by the way the Johnson administration handled the war.

Campus opinion is virtually unanimous that Johnson made a major historical error in refusing to agree at an earlier date to a bombing halt. The pleas of U Thant, the considered opinions of politicians in both campus, and the prodding from intellectual groups on the campuses were ample evidence to the students that peace negotiations might have been undertaken sooner and the war might have been terminated at an earlier date had the president acted unilaterally during any one of several opportunities made available to him.

Surprisingly enough, students do not want us to pull out unilaterally even now. The students were asked this question first: "Do you believe the United States made a mistake in sending troops to Vietnam?" Sixty percent of all students said yes, 37 percent said no, with 3 percent not sure or having no answer.

Students were then asked: "Regardless of your previous answer, what should we do today?" Fifty-eight percent of those queried felt that we should de-escalate; less than 27 percent recommended escalation to victory. But only 15 percent said we should pull out regardless of the results of the negotiations. It is obvious, therefore, that the college generation recognizes that we should live up to our commitments once they are given.

Students especially resent the apparent lack of participation by the South Vietnamese. Public statements that American youths were dying while South Vietnamese youths had not even been drafted were played up prominently in school newspapers and campus rallies. Robert Kennedy's stand on this issue was a key reason for his campus popularity.

In the months leading up to the 1968 elections and prior to the withdrawal of President Johnson, the seeming obstinacy on the part of the federal administration, coupled with the complete ineptness of the South Vietnamese Army, was doubtlessly the cause of much of the campus fury and frustration with the war—a handy circumstance exploited by radicals. The reporting of the facts of the war also tended to create a credibility gap between the campus and the government. Statements by a succession of government officials to the effect that the war was going well, falsely optimistic reports on battlefield progress by army commanders, and contradictory stories filed by war correspondents all tended to create disbelief in the minds of the college students as to the honesty of the government in its official pronouncements and confusion about the real state of affairs.

It is unfair to charge the college generation with unwillingness to assume responsibility for military duty. The College Poll clearly shows that students recognize their obligation of defending their country. The difference between the current attitude and that of previous generations in this area might best be explained by saying that today's students want to know "why." As for their courage and ability under fire, assurances given the various governments, are basically un-military field commanders have admitted many times that the current generation is the equivalent of the American soldier in the best traditions of our history.

One method by which students express their dissatisfaction with the war is by accentuating the inequities in the draft. The College Poll figures reveal that most students would not use illegal means to avoid the draft, including such drastic methods as burning their draft cards or even going to Canada. In addition, draft boards are generally regarded as fair as they can be under the rules and regulations set down by the Selective Service Act.

Students did indicate, however, their clear-cut conviction that the draft itself is basically unfair, particularly in the method by which deferments are given. They resent the cancellation of the graduate deferments, which they felt was a penalty against a particular segment of the college community. They also believe the draft law is prejudicial to the blacks and the poor who are unable to attend college. In other words, the social consciousness of American students—many of whom come from above-average-income families—carried no intrinsic pleasure in their military free status at the expense of less fortunate members of the same generation.

The College Poll reveals undergraduate resentment of the press coverage of the draft riots on college campuses, in newspapers, magazines, and on television—all of which gave the impression that this was an ungrateful and cowardly generation, unwilling to bear its responsibilities as citizens. Actually the draft-card incidents were conducted by a handful of radicals with whom most students had no sympathy.

Campus opinion is very much in favor of a volunteer army and the abolition of the draft. In fact, students await President Nixon's action on this measure—a campaign stand of the Republican President—as an indication of the administration's follow-through on pre-election promises. His proposal of a lottery is not accepted by most students as any real solution to draft inequities.

Incidentally, university sentiment against the draft has always been strong though it has often been overshadowed by other campus issues. Past College Poll studies showed that most students regarded the draft as unfair. The question was asked again after President Nixon's election, "Do you think the present draft system is fair?" Seventy-seven percent of all students still said no.

"President Nixon knew the students were for a volunteer army—and he used it to get student support," declared a Cal Tech junior. "Now that he's in power, let's see what he does about it."

"Draft reform and a volunteer army are pretty far down the list of government priorities these days," said a Tulane sophomore. "It's just about what I expected."

This question was then asked of students: "Should we have

a volunteer army and do away with the draft?" Of all students interviewed 65 percent said yes.

Students favoring the volunteer system feel that enough men would respond to the ranks of the armed forces to meet any emergency.

"Look at the ROTC," said a Harvard senior. "That's largely a volunteer program. By being made attractive, the program is all filled up."

"The draft causes most of the troubles with the youth today. It's used as a threat over the heads of everybody," said a CCNY junior. "If the Army had to go out and get its men by inducement rather than by induction, it would be even a better army."

Although all graduations of attitude appeared in answer to the queries of College Poll field representatives, the consensus of opinion among the vast body of those interviewed was that a volunteer-army program would "take the pressure" off the college generation.

"The enforced draft is a mixed-up series of regulations that change with the whim of General Hershey," said a Vanderbilt senior.

A Buffalo U. sophomore felt that "there are plenty of Americans who would volunteer—even those who resist the draft—if it was not mandatory. There should be some changes in the length of duty, and certainly in the pay of the volunteers."

"If they'd end the Vietnam War, the volunteer army would be filled up overnight," a Houston senior was quoted as saying.

"A draft army lets the government have a ready force to move any time it wants. If they had to encourage volunteers, the decisions as to interference in the affairs of other nations might be made more carefully. This does not apply, of course, in cases of attack or aggression by other nations that affect our security," said a Columbia senior.

Those opposed to a volunteer army preferred traditional arguments. "It won't work. It's hard to get students by draft. How are we going to get them by volunteering?"

"It's undemocratic," stated a Yale freshman. "Men of all income backgrounds should bear the responsibility for defense. A volunteer army becomes a poor man's army—and that's undemocratic."

"The danger lies in over-militarism," commented a Villanova senior. "A volunteer army becomes a career army. We have to be careful of a career-army control in this country, as President Eisenhower pointed out."

The election of President Nixon and the opening of peace talks in Paris served to cool much of the anger toward both the Vietnam situation and the draft. So long as the peace talks progress it is unlikely that either the draft or Vietnam will be used as focal points for further campus unrest. Student radicals have shifted their emphasis to the ROTC and the military establishment. But the war is an ever-present and ominous cloud upon the campuses of America, and the draft, unless it is revised, remains as a daily reminder to students that service in Vietnam is only as far away as the next report card.

Student attitudes are not all negative and probably are not that much different from those of American society in general. They hope that the new administration will be able to create a greater rapport with them as far as the war in Vietnam is concerned.

On the whole, students view with quiet skepticism the progress of the talks in Paris. They regard the technical delays in Paris as ludicrous and are more interested in what our representatives are doing than in what the Vietnamese are attempting to accomplish. It is unfortunate but true that American college students are inclined to question the good faith and credibility of U. S. representatives. For example, Henry Cabot Lodge unfortunately is viewed by many students as one of the architects of duplicity in helping to get rid of a Saigon government. On the one hand, students hope we will take the initiative on negotiations, initiate concessions, create compromises, and find a solution to the impasses that repeatedly occur. On the other hand, there is also an unwillingness to face the fact that Hanoi is a ruthless and calculating enemy that exploits weaknesses, including the lack of confidence that the college generation has given to the federal administration.

Meanwhile, the undergraduate community is deeply concerned about future commitments that could involve us in confrontations similar to Vietnam, and its members have definite ideas on how to avoid such situations.

Asked whether we should send troops "elsewhere," students answered as follows:

Only for national defense	59%
Never for another Vietnam	25%
Under no circumstances	16%

Students were then questioned in particular about the Middle East. Many say it could become another Vietnam. We are backing Israel. Russia is backing the Arabs. What should we do?

Students voted 60 percent to 33 percent not to back Israel. Seven percent had no opinion.

"We shouldn't get into that position on either side," said an NYU junior.

"In the event Israel was attacked, should we back them with armed intervention?" students were asked. Fifty percent of all students said no.

"We should tell both sides, including Russia, we won't fight. That's what will help keep us out" was the emphatic opinion of a Harvard junior.

"The Israelis want us to fight to protect their borders," said an Alabama senior, obviously unhappy about the continuing Middle East tensions.

"It's a typical situation. Nobody really understands it. I'm not sure Israel is right or wrong—but we should never lose one American life over a grudge fight like the Arabs against the Jews," declared a St. Louis U. student.

In passing, it is interesting to note that most students were convinced that Russia would not fight either.

What would most college students do about the problem?

"We should keep these fights in the UN. That's one of the functions for which the UN was founded," said a Northwestern sophomore. Sixty-five percent of all students agreed with him.

We should also keep negotiations going with Russia to help maintain the peace.

Questioned specifically about the United Nations, the great majority of collegians agreed that it is the best hope for world peace.

In summation, students want the U.S. to avoid unilateral world commitments except in defense of our nation.

The top priority is the Vietnam War and the draft. Peace on the campus may depend to a great extent on how these two issues are handled by the current administration.

CHAPTER FOUR

The College Student Looks at Sex

"Sex is beautiful."

No other expression of the general attitude of the college generation toward sex is more descriptive or more frank. The word "beautiful" may have various shades of meaning, but whether it is used in the hep sense or as a mere adjective in the usual connotation, to most college students sex is natural, beautiful, accepted, open, and a necessary fact of life.

And if parents are at a loss to understand the extent and nature of the generation gap, the area of sex and the student's love life is a classic example.

"My mother and father never used the word 'sex' in my presence in my whole life," reported a Tulane junior to a College Poll interviewer. "I can't imagine my ever bringing up the subject at home. In fact, we never referred to our bodies by the medical terms. My mother and father always lived their lives as if physical love and sex never existed."

The following is typical.

"I get a kick out of my father trying to tell me about how to treat girls, and how not to get into trouble," commented a Kent State sophomore. "He really doesn't know how much I know, and he's so embarrassed about the subject."

"My mother tries to have a real heart-to-heart talk with me about boys and what they are like," observed a Ladycliff junior. "Good Lord, I knew more as a high school sophomore than she's trying to tell me. She means well, but Mom is about ten years behind the scene."

Sex and the facts of life are not strange or embarrassing to most students. The college generation has been raised in an atmosphere of physical frankness their parents never knew. College girls and boys have learned the nature of each other's bodies and cultivated an ease of physical contact that is foreign to the older generation. Most parents would be confounded if they eavesdropped on a conversation among four or five college students packed into a booth at a local pub debating the merits and demerits of the pill.

Discussions on abortion laws, premarital sex, divorce and its causes, homosexuality, and physiological aberrations are often frank and commonplace among students of both sexes.

And it is not all talk. The practice of premarital sex is widespread on the campus, according to the College Poll interviewers. Almost three out of four students believe that most young men and women attending universities engage in sexual relations before marriage.

Students were asked this question: "Dr. Kinsey is reported to have said that nearly two-thirds of all college students engage in premarital sexual relations, or intercourse. Do you believe this is true?"

Among all individuals questioned, 74.8 percent said they believe it to be true; 25.2 percent said it was untrue. The opinions of coeds and males were almost the same.

"Yes, I think it is true, from what I know about it," said a Northwestern coed, voicing an opinion held by many of her college sisters.

"What's the big deal, even if it's true? After all, this is 1969," insisted a University of Southern California sophomore. Although not in the same words, his reaction spells out the opinion of most college men. While some may hedge personally, students find little disagreement with the concept.

"This is not to say it applies to me—but from what I hear in the dorm, I'd say it's true," said a Cornell coed.

"Kinsey was wrong—it's higher," insisted a Washington State junior.

Those who disagree feel quite strongly. "All talk," said a Bowdoin sophomore. And a Louisiana State sophomore added, "I doubt it's that high. There are a lot of talkers and not too many doers."

But the real reaction comes from those individuals who believe what they or their classmates do is their business. As adults, they resent hypocrisy about sex and sexual relations.

"If a guy goes with a girl for a year or so, whose business is it what goes on? It's their lives and if they want love, it's up to them to decide" was the attitude of a Boston sophomore.

"It's no worse than it was in the days of my parents—except nobody was counting in those days" was the way many students spoke out.

"What are you supposed to do if you're going steady— hold hands?" curtly asked an Oregon State senior.

Students do not place the lack of virginity—either male or female—as a deterrent in their eyes as a potential factor in choosing a mate. Students were asked the question: "Would you marry a girl who is no longer a virgin?"

Seventy-three percent of all men said yes, 21 percent said no, and the remaining students refused to answer or were undecided.

"Of course, I'd rather she were," said a Tufts senior, "but if I loved her, I'd marry her and forget the past."

"We have to face life as it is—not as it was," declared a Richmond sophomore. "Girls get around today, and who's to say they are any less worthy wives and mothers for it?"

The minority view is that of a University of Virginia sophomore.

"Sure I know what goes on, but the girl I marry wouldn't have been involved that way."

As might be expected, students' ideas change the longer they are in school. Thirty-eight percent of freshmen thought virginity was important. By the time they were seniors, only 8 percent felt it was an important factor in selecting a lifetime mate. On the other hand, Catholics held to a more traditional view. Only 66 percent of Catholics said they would marry a nonvirgin, whereas 85 percent of the Protestants felt it made no difference.

Coeds are also much more realistic than the public might believe. There is no "double standard" on the campus, according to the College Poll. Seven out of ten coeds answered yes when asked: "Would you marry a man whom you knew has had sexual relations with other unmarried girls?" Twenty-one percent said no or weren't sure. The others gave no answer.

"I suppose most men have had sex with girls at one time or another," said a Buffalo University coed. "It's what he feels about me that counts."

"If you lived on campus for four years as I have, nothing shocks you," commented a Syracuse senior journalism major. "But when love comes along, the past is shut out."

"I would wonder, I guess," said a pretty auburn-haired Oregon State senior. "I'd rather I was first."

This sophisticated attitude toward sex of the college generation is the result of a sexual orientation that started early in their lives. Products of the *Playboy* age through exposure to sex in motion pictures, magazines, advertisements —students, both male and female, have stripped away most of the mystery and reserve with which their parents view sex.

Social relations on the campus are freer than ever before. The automobile, the nearby motel, and the mixed weekend all bring students into close physical contact, providing, at the same time, the opportunity for a fuller exploration of intimate emotional relationships. Students are less inhibited in kissing and petting. It all goes back to students feeling that they are, in fact, adults, and having adult physical and emotional reactions, expect they will be accepted as such.

Much of the conflict with campus authorities arises from a lack of agreement on this subject. The rules prohibiting males from visiting females in their dormitory rooms, and vice versa, have been under attack on most campuses. It's a popular issue. Most students feel the rules are archaic and unrealistic in terms of our contemporary mores.

When asked, "Do you believe unmarried students should be allowed to entertain members of the opposite sex in their college rooms?", nine out of ten students replied yes.

"Why not? Aren't we supposed to be adults?" inquired an Indiana junior.

Some, however, agree to some qualifications—"only if the door is open" (from a Wisconsin co-ed), and "yes if there's more than one other present" (a Denver junior).

But most students consider it more of a right than a privilege.

"When schools forbid visiting between students of different sexes, it shows they don't trust their students," declared a North Carolina senior.

Nor does the average undergraduate feel it will lead to more sexual relations.

"If we want hanky-panky, we don't need a college room," said a Radcliffe sophomore. "Where there's a will, there's a way. Room visiting is not the same at all."

Nor is the reason only social—it has some economic soundness.

"If I have to take a girl out on a date every time I see her, I'd go broke," said a Pitt junior. "You can't go to the library or take a walk all the time! There's no reason I can't have her up for an evening, except for some stupid rules made years ago when girls had to have chaperons."

"I can't see why I can't have a date in my room," said a Barnard senior. "I was always allowed to have boys in my home. My mother and father welcomed them. What better way to find out what a boy is like than seeing him in your own place? If my room at college is my home, I should be able to have him in. After all, I'll probably be married next year."

The issue has brought many changes. Yale and scores of other schools have changed their rules. In other locations, campus proctors have become more tolerant, but greater leniency is not enough for most students. They want the rules changed so they are more consistent with realistic changes occurring in other aspects of campus life. Compromises have taken place on some campuses—with visiting rules being extended until midnight and male visitors being allowed to visit female dormitories during the week.

All this new and increased demand for freedom does not imply that the student is more promiscuous, or that the college campus has become a place for a gigantic orgy.

"There is no evidence that students are more sexually indiscriminate than their parents," stated a Michigan psychology professor. "The evidence seems clear that the student treats sex as part of a whole relationship with his or her partner. It becomes meaningful in their lives. There is even some evidence that it promotes a greater maturity in these relationships by the elimination of sex and sexual gratification as the sole reason for their continuance."

Students may make love to those close to them, and feel little guilt as a result, the College Poll seems to indicate. This "loose" sense of morality does not imply carrying on insincere relationships. Immorality is more a definition of sexual license than sexual fulfillment to today's college student.

There is no longer the fear of sexual relations that inhibited previous generations. Students are familiar with all forms of contraceptives and find them readily available. The pill, which normally requires a medical prescription, can be obtained from a number of sources, including friends, relatives, and sympathetic druggists and physicians. In addition, abortions are readily available—either locally or in nearby cities. Students attach little moral stigma to abortions. Many consider it to be a "better way out" or "the lesser of two evils." Most girls prefer abortions to having a child and turning it over for adoption—a process that requires dropping out of school and parental knowledge or consent. Abortions can be secured over a weekend—at a cost of $500 or less, plus transportation. Dormitory friends frequently "chip in" for such emergencies.

It is this firsthand knowledge of abortion that prompts students to seek a change in the abortion laws. Most students believe that abortion laws are hypocritical. While no factual estimate of the real number of abortions performed on college girls exists, at least one out of ten students says he has "heard of" a schoolmate who had an abortion. These young men and women recommend that the laws be changed to permit abortions for unmarrieds. Nor do they believe such a move would lead to sexual promiscuity.

Student attitudes to the flood of sexually oriented material that permeates the market today also provides some revealing reactions. When asked: "Do you think there is too much pornography available to the youth today?", most students answered no.

"Everybody talks about pornography, but even the Supreme Court can't define it," commented a Lehigh sophomore.

"*Playboy* started it all," commented a University of Detroit student. "It was Hugh Hefner who pulled the veil off hypocrisy in sex and the human body."

It probably is true. *Playboy* is a virtual dormitory bible. *Playboy* calendars, pinups, and the inevitable "center-fold" art are prominent all over the campus. The "body beautiful" is no longer a subject of furtive viewing.

Nor are students shocked at the freewheeling sex literature

that crams the best-seller lists. In fact, it's this very public acceptance of lurid literature that students regard as another indication of "hypocrisy" and dishonesty in laws.

"It's not we students who pay seven dollars for *Portnoy's Complaint*," commented a Stanford junior. "It's the ladies of the bridge club who make these books best sellers because they want to read all the dirty words."

Or, as another Fordham student explained the same thought, "Sure we read *Playboy*, and we're not ashamed of it. It has some great girls and good articles. But we get a kick out of the old guys who hide it under their *Wall Street Journal!*"

Although there is little to be shocked about in literature, there is a growing concern on the campus about motion-picture frankness.

"It's going too far," stated a Penn State coed. "These days, it's embarrassing to go to the films with a date."

It's really not the frankness that disturbs most of the college generation. Accustomed to nudity or near-nudity in beachwear, students are generally not offended by films that display the female body or generous portions of the male physique. But they are quick to react to bad taste or cheap films.

"Nudity is one thing," added a Santa Fe junior, "but explicit sex is generally in bad taste."

The Graduate was the most popular film on the campus last year. Although it treated certain aspects of love and sex with frankness, students felt it was "real" and in good taste. They still rave over *A Man and a Woman,* a film that has been rerun extensively on campus. But hard-core stag films have no general popularity with the college generation. The run-of-the-mill imported sex films find little audience on the campus. Again the students sense a hypocrisy in their elders in this respect.

"You don't see college kids paying $3.50 to see *I Am*

Curious (Yellow)," said a Temple junior. "Look at the lines in front of the theater and you'll see the dirty old men paying to see it."

Students are avid motion-picture fans. A good number of them go to the movies several times a month, the College Poll shows. Many colleges have their own theaters, where major films are regularly exhibited. It is on the campus where the art films—the imported pictures from Italy, France, Sweden, and other countries—have reached their greatest popularity. Names like Fellini, Bergman, and Antonioni are well known to most undergraduates. While many of these films portray frank presentations of life, to students they are true art pictures, much different from the "grind" films seen in local towns.

In addition, many colleges have film societies and film courses. More than 250 feature films are produced yearly by campus producers, who conduct their own film festivals and film awards. Well-made, in color, and with excellent photography (but generally weak scripts), these films are circulated on the campus network.

Major film companies understand the value of the campus audience who, by word-of-mouth promotion, can make or break a picture. Thus the current concern for frankness in major films by students themselves may prove a backlash to Hollywood studios.

All in all, the college student has a healthy attitude toward sex and life. He feels he is more honest about it than his parents. He accepts sex as a fact of life and a binding force in personal relationships, not a substitute for lack of communication between people. They are, on the whole, both amused and annoyed by parental bewilderment by these attitudes. They feel well equipped in this area to face life—better, in fact, then their parents and other elders. It is the failure on the part of the older generation to recognize this adult attitude toward sex and life that creates much of the friction between the ages. On campus, it results in dissatisfaction with rules and regulations that treat students as children and the school as a parent.

Much of the sex and love life of contemporary college people is based on a "now" attitude toward life. While many students traditionally look forward to their existence in the future—a home and children—the pervading atmosphere on campus is "now." They are adults—in love—and life is here and now. Rather than face the hypocrisy of ignoring the depths of their emotions or hoping for a future that may never arrive, and freed from moral and medical restrictions that provided outdated sanctions, today's college students face sex frankly and honestly.

Love is not all sex, however. Students still walk the university quadrangles holding hands. They still meet in libraries, "at the door next to the cafeteria," or "over at Brescia Hall," as they have for generations. The telephones on all floors are always busy, and on weekends the exodus to nearby girls' colleges, or the city, is in full swing. College card shops do a brisk business in valentines and friendship cards, and campus bull sessions in men's and women's dormitories mostly center (after the subject of Vietnam) on girl-and-boy talk.

College deans state frankly that "involvement with members of the opposite sex" is an all-too-frequent cause for the freshman or sophomore dropout. In short, students still fall in love.

Most women expect to be married "within one year after graduation," the College Poll reports. Men, however, don't expect to get married until "three or more years after college." Girls and boys both consider it "probable" that they will marry someone they meet in college. In fact, students—especially coeds—admit that "social reasons" were a principal factor in their selection of the college they attended—and that availability of members of the opposite sex was a prime

And it's precisely for this reason—the basic calm and rationality of the average student—that there is little actual violence on the campus today.

Then why are there riots at all? What causes the disgruntled but docile student to break out into violent action with seeming readiness? For it must be true that in the Columbia, Harvard, Cornell, and Berkeley riots, a large segment of the student population was involved at those campuses. In San Francisco State University, a unique situation, there were at one time nearly a thousand storming the police on the campus.

To understand what takes place on these troubled campuses, it is important to understand the composition of the students involved. First, on each of these campuses, there is a hard-core student activist organization. There must be no misunderstanding as to the nature of this group. They are dedicated radicals. On some campuses, like Columbia and San Francisco State, they can become virtual anarchists. They have little faith in democratic society, and therefore no confidence in its institutions. Unable to change society as a whole, they concentrate on the university—the world in which they live. The key group in this activity is the Students for a Democratic Society, commonly called the S.D.S. Founded in 1962 by about 50 students from 11 colleges at a meeting at Port Huron, Michigan, it has grown into 350 chapters with approximately 70,000 members.

At Port Huron, it formulated a program—"democracy of individual action." Its impact has been beyond the wildest dreams of its membership. Its militancy has created student strikes, sit-ins, mass rallies, and finally riots that have been the principal cause of the image of upheaval that surrounds the campus today. In this year, the Port Huron plan has reached a climax. It was the S.D.S. that spurred the San Francisco State University riot, the Harvard outbreak, and the Columbia strikes. It is tied in with another group called the Mao Progressive Labor party—a more militant and radical campus organization linked with radical groups throughout the world.

The S.D.S. is operated out of Chicago where a trio of national officers acts as a coordinating committee. Primarily, however, the S.D.S. is a loosely held group of local organizations. The local chapters are of varying strength and impact, depending upon the skill and dedication of its leaders. Mark Rudd, the Columbia S.D.S. leader, was a skillful organizer who gained national fame from wide newspaper and television coverage. Others, not so well known, do a remarkable job organizing their dedicated middle-class students into hard action on popular issues.

There are other groups, the MOBE or the National Mobilization Committee to End the Vietnam War—which coordinated the protesting groups at the Chicago Democratic Convention. The Resistance is a group that began primarily to break the draft and led the card-burning, sit-down efforts that gained so much publicity. In recent months its members, dedicated radicals all, joined hands with some black groups to exploit civil rights issues on the campus. But usually blacks reject white interference with their movement.

The graduate students and teachers have their own radical groups—a very small but powerful minority on the campus. The largest of these—the New University Conference, has chapters on nearly one hundred campuses. This group works closely with student radical groups—coordinating demands against the administrations on key issues, and providing confrontations within faculty groups themselves. These faculty committees, often set up as the result of students' demands, are in turn subject to intellectual harangues that exploit the teacher's own dissatisfactions with the administration, thus compounding the confusion and chaos.

These groups are united in one area. They are convinced that change must come—not small change—but a basic readjustment of our social and economic order.

"It's not only a sick society—it's a rotten society. It must be changed from top to bottom, and start by tearing it apart," said an S.D.S. leader.

One need only to listen to the diatribe of Mark Rudd to see that little reason is applied or considered in the campus confrontations.

The university is the tool of a weak society, the radical activists claim. It is the university that wages war through its defense contracts. It is the university that wages war against the poor and oppressed by taking away the homes of the Negroes adjacent to Columbia to build a gym—and in Boston, by Harvard wiping out slum apartments owned by the university. It is the university, that by grants from industry, debases the teachers and professors, perpetuating the Establishment and the system.

Against this background, the radicals say reason won't work. Compromise is not practical.

"The system is too rotten," said a radical Columbia student. "Mere token change means nothing. We have to take over the university."

In 1969 the S.D.S. conducted a "spring offensive" against the American university. Choosing issues carefully according to location, the S.D.S. exhibits surprising strength because its objectives and complaints closely parallel student attitudes. For example, at Columbia, the local race issue—the university taking over the poor-black house—was a complaint that won the sympathy of the student body at large. Its demands are usually set forth with considerable skill and slanted in the interest of justice while highlighting the plight of the depressed and oppressed. It fights "militarism," "the Vietnam War," "racism," and presses for greater control by students —all issues with which students can agree in principal—and that gain the support of many faculty members as well.

The procedure for starting confrontation is fairly standard. The committee sets a date, prepares the posters, cards, and leaflets, and picks a focal point on the campus for maximum exposure. In some cases, seizure and sit-ins are used to help dramatize the confrontation.

Recently, picking on a sympathetic issue or two—the ROTC, the displacement of black people in Chicago, or poor housing at Harvard—the radicals create a "non-negotiable" issue with the college administration, and, using at first nonviolent means, try to force police action to repress their activities. Up to this stage, few students actively back their actions, although many agree with their complaints. In fact, even in the early stages of all these demonstrations, the student body on the whole is at best apathetic toward the activists.

Where does the breaking point come?—Usually with the advent of the local police.

"There's nothing like having the police break a few heads of their classmates to shake students out of their apathy," said an S.D.S. organizer with a smile on his face.

"The sight of blood caused by the blows from the police pigs is usually enough to get it really rolling," commented a Columbia activist. "That sets up the sides pretty fast and we're off and running."

To students who object to the uses of violence, the bringing in of outside police *is* violence. Usually it produces violence, and violence directed especially against the campus.

The result does, in fact, polarize the students. They then feel it is the administration that causes and uses violence. Generally, along with the confrontation go statements and charges by the radicals that, in the heat of the fracas, produce other charges. Contradictory statements by harassed administration officials more often than not result in an increased credibility gap between students and college officials. Often, in an attempt to reduce tensions, campus officials make concessions that they hope never to have to fulfill.

It is these elements that swing apathetic students into action. Students resent outside pressures and invariably take the side of their colleagues in such riots. The pattern is not accidental. The riots are carefully planned, expertly executed, and with a finesse gained by success and experience.

These riots are more successful in the large city areas, where local radicals infiltrate the campus to aid in the organization and execution of the campaign. Moreover, the large urban college is usually more committed in the area of civil rights issues. In addition, they have larger administrative units, which result in more impersonal contact with students.

The riots have not helped the dialogue between the generations, in the opinion of most students.

Many students realize that they have been put on the defensive in trying to bring about reform or explain their ideas. Parents and legislators, concerned about the growing lawlessness and disorder, have taken a less sympathetic attitude toward student opinion.

"My father thinks all rioters should be jailed or thrown out of school," commented a Vassar student. "He won't listen to any arguments about the way a school should be changed at all now."

Are riots likely to continue? Probably, for as long as the radical element remains on the campus and feels that violence is a way of creating change and attention, confrontations will continue.

"All I know is that what we are doing today about racism and war and the American society is what radicals should be doing" was the frank statement of a Northwestern radical S.D.S. leader.

The whole area of black-white relations has explosive potential—more serious and more deeply rooted than even many college officials realize.

But the atmosphere is changing. At first, campus officials were hardly prepared for the intensity of the guerrilla warfare the radicals used. College presidents, faculty members, and trustees were shocked into virtual helplessness and the radicals exploited this weakness to good effect. But that, too, is changing. College officials are now better prepared for potential trouble and have well-laid plans to control the groups. Many, like the MIT administration, have anticipated student demands and stolen the thunder from radical claims.

"The college has co-opted us at every turn," said S.D.S. leaders at MIT.

Colleges have learned to use the law and not fight it. By the proper use of court orders and injunctions, university officials have found a way to make rioting illegal. Students are "restrained" from illegal acts by court orders. If they violate these orders, they become in contempt of court and are properly and promptly sent to jail—not for rioting—but for violation of court orders. Jail sentences can be stiff. Dartmouth radicals were shocked at the thirty-day sentences meted out at Hanover this spring.

Students back these moves. The College Poll shows that most students—80 percent—feel that students who break the law in campus fights should be arrested and expelled.

There is evidence that students themselves are fed up with the demonstrations. When asked, "Are you getting tired of all the campus unrest?" 62 percent of the students answered yes.

Students are deeply concerned with the loss of class hours as a result of demonstrations, often over issues with which they have increasingly less interest. CCNY students were bitter over the lengthy cancellation of classes last spring. A Harvard student threatened to sue dissident groups if he failed his courses as a result of the strike.

Moreover, there is no broad national issue that arouses students like the draft and Vietnam did in the past two years. Most demonstrations about the ROTC and war contracts now fail to excite students except in key schools like Harvard and Columbia, the S.D.S. has found.

The schools and the law have gone on the offensive as well, striking directly at the radical groups. It is not too well known that police units have actually infiltrated into the S.D.S. and have the groups under constant surveillance. An indication of this activity is the fact that when Mark Rudd was arrested at Columbia, the arresting officer was his bodyguard—a police undercover agent who had become Rudd's buddy during the hot period. There is little the FBI doesn't know about the radicals, and federal officials watch the activities of the leaders, especially when they travel around the country. While not harassment, this activity does inhibit the whole movement. It is particularly effective in alienating fringe radicals who are not dedicated and who fear jail terms or police records.

Many liberals have turned away from the S.D.S. campaigns, mostly because of their irrational tactics. The thrust of S.D.S. activity thus seems to be more directed at industry and high schools—where there is less organization against them and a greater opportunity for introducing guerrilla tactics. In the summer of 1969, the S.D.S. tried to organize students to disrupt plants at their summer jobs. With booklets and pamphlets covering "how-to" directions, the radicals urged students to get into small businesses, largely with black help and start demonstrations. The *Wall Street Journal* learned of this through the FBI and published warnings to businesses to beware of college help. Many undergraduates found difficulty in getting jobs, due to this activity.

Students also realize that the riots have produced some strange bedfellows. Although most students do not feel that there is a "Communist conspiracy" in connection with the college riots, when asked if the riots were supported by Communists, 44 percent of all interviewed felt that activists got "some help" from the Communists. Students fear that such associations will hurt, not help, campus reforms.

"All we need now is to start a campus witch-hunt," said a

Cornell sophomore. "If they prove the Communists are connected with the riots, there will be a congressional investigation and the works. They'd never leave us alone."

This feeling that the whole project may have gotten out of hand is shared by many students.

"'All we wanted was to bring girls to our rooms,'" commented a Columbia sophomore. "We got a war instead."

Students still want change, however. In the spring of 1969, the College Poll found that 61 percent were still not satisfied with the way their colleges were administered.

Nor do students feel they should run away from a school they don't like. Many parents have taken the stand that "if you don't like the way a school is run, you should go someplace else." Most students reject that position—72 percent said they don't agree to such a statement. Students feel that change is universal, that they have a duty to make their views felt.

"There would never be any change if the students didn't speak out" is how one concerned young coed put it.

But much has occurred on the campus that has reduced the need for violence.

The riots have had some positive results, and it is in the fact that they have brought positive action that the danger lies.

In a survey conducted in the spring of 1969, the College. Poll noticed that students still opposed violence by a large vote—80 percent were against any form of violence. But it was in the comments even by those who opposed it that a new attitude was apparent.

"One fact is that it made the colleges listen to students," said a UCLA junior. "Not that I recommend it, but we certainly wouldn't have had all these changes otherwise."

"It brought the needed attention and stress to the problem," a University of Colorado sophomore commented.

"We found that a polite request got a polite 'no,'" said a

Dickinson junior. "I wouldn't like any more, but it did get results."

"If nonviolence is met by violence, violence must be reciprocated," said a Washington University sophomore.

"Violence has been a main cause of social change throughout history," commented a Lowell Tech junior. "It seems to have done some good on the campus this year—bad as it is."

And student attitudes are well founded. Vast changes in opinion have, indeed, occurred on the campus scene as a result of the confrontations. Radical students who have achieved notoriety and success far beyond their expectations, credit the riots and willingness to risk violence as the real reason for their success.

As a result of their actions, they have seen college administrators shocked into broad and almost overnight reforms of campus life. On hundreds of campuses, student-faculty forums have been established. In many instances, students are being appointed to committees to meet with faculty on classroom problems. Students have joined deans in discussing curriculum changes. In some instances, students are being considered for appointment to boards of trustees in advisory positions.

A broad dialogue has, indeed, been started on the campus. College officials have become concerned about student demands, needs, and interests. This makes radicalism less necessary, and confrontations less likely. In this atmosphere, students themselves resent interruptions on the campus where the hope of action is held out.

One of the least publicized casualties of the campus revolt may well turn out to be the news media. The extent to which the credibility and goodwill of the nation's newspapers, magazines, television, and radio have been discredited in the eyes of the college generation is one of the best-kept secrets of the period.

The average college student is both bewildered and irritated by the "overkill" of the American press coverage of the campus activities.

It must be remembered that, to the college student, his demands for reforms, for relevancy, for reframing of his university were sincere appeals made to perpetrate the university, not to destroy it. To most students, violence was never conceived, let alone condoned. They expected confrontations and eventual discussion and compromise. They rejected extreme radicalism of any kind and were dismayed by the turmoil that has resulted. Many are in agreement that the American press intruded into the campus scene and turned an internal discussion into a national scandal, giving it a prominence that was entirely unwarranted.

Admittedly, most students have been well aware that the militant groups have used the press to achieve their ends, while the press has, in turn, used the militants to feed headlines that never reflected the real attitudes of collegians.

The extent to which the newspapers, television, and radio cooperated with the radicals and helped to stage and exploit the confrontations is a story most students would like told. It is recognized on the campuses that the activists have an awareness of the value of the press and publicity media. Student activists are taught how to gather headlines and are masters of the use of media. Activists are quick to get appointed to college newspapers, establish an underground press, seek control of campus radios. It must also be remembered that most students are tolerant of such activities. Activists customarily use areas of reform with which most students agree as the basis of their arguments. What is frequently misunderstood is that the great majority of university males and females do not agree either with the activists' solutions to those problems, or the means they use to solve them.

The news media have made no such distinction, students told the College Poll interviewers. In fact, they believe that the reporting of the campus revolution has been inaccurate if not dishonest. The results are a disheartening lack of sympathy for real areas of reform, and an overall condemnation of the college generation as violent, unreasoning, and ruthless, with neither purpose nor control.

The resentment of the college student is deep and may well be long lasting. They watched the press cooperate with student rioters at Berkeley, Harvard, Columbia, Brandeis, the University of Connecticut, San Francisco State, CCNY, and other schools to get coverage. There was coordination between rioters and the press to be sure that coverage was arranged. Press coverage was always "available" for the Mark Rudd press conferences. The handling of the campus riots by television cameras was done with the same skill with which the cameras covered the Rose Bowl football games. Television cameras just don't arrive on campus. They are cumbersome, huge caravans requiring large amounts of electricity and complex logistics.

Television cameramen, with their harnesses, and news photographers using light meters and color photography covered every confrontation with preparation and skill, using background shots, crowd shots, and close-ups of screaming rioters. The resultant pictures and film made immediate headlines. Plans for the next confrontation were discussed freely with the news media. Press covered the police plans, and were ready with camera and film when the clashes occurred.

Most students resent the coverage because it neither represents campus consensus, nor was the coverage equally balanced. Without denying that all involved bear some blame for the riots, the press is not without its own measure of responsibility.

The following quotations are representative of collegiate opinion in this area:

"If this is the way the press covers everything, I wonder how accurately they cover other topics of the day."

"I wonder if we are really getting the true story of Vietnam."

"Mayor Daly was right. The press creates the atmosphere that radicals exploit."

"It's almost vicious. When television says anything, people take it as gospel."

"I never realized the power of the press before—and how irresponsibly they use it."

"These radicals would be no place today if the press didn't make them heroes. Mark Rudd is no more a spokesman for the college generation than Rapp Brown is a spokesman for the blacks. But the *New York Times* made him a national figure."

"Why don't they leave us alone? With all the troubles in the world today, why don't they send their cameras into the slums we are trying to get rid of?"

"The press, not the radicals, forced the president to resign."

"Television scares me. They've made a war out of a complaint."

"Don't investigate S.D.S. Investigate CBS."

"The press forced Governor Reagan to make angry statements and take a stand. He had to—he's a politician. But nothing gets solved."

"Last week the whole *New York Times* was covered with campus stories. Every college where a student raised his voice was all over the papers. Now I ask you, what happens about all the murders that go on that day, or the hundreds of divorces, or the forgery cases, or the other crimes? They have played up the campus riots because they make news. It's terrible."

"The nation's newspapers have blackballed the whole college generation."

"Campus radicals are like brats. They only create tantrums when people watch them. The television cameras have given them a wonderful audience, thus enabling them to be brats in front of the whole country. Now try to stop them."

"I called my mother the day after the Dartmouth arrests. They were nothing up here at school. But she said it was all over the *New York Times*. I was furious. They made a big riot out of a small incident, which half the campus knew nothing about. Dartmouth deserves more than that."

However some students may feel about college administrators, most feel deep sympathy for harassed presidents who were badgered by reporters into statements that were probably ill thought out, and were sensationalized all out of context. This, in turn, produced additional well-publicized retorts by activists, and a whole new cycle of "news." Faculty members themselves, torn between loyalty and progress, were sought out by reporters and photographers and goaded into statements that hardly reflected reasoned judgments, coming as they did in the arena-like atmosphere. Many will long bear the scars of publicity that they ill deserve. On the other hand, radical faculty members became good copy to the press and helped fan the fires on the campus. In the meantime, the press fanned out.

It must be remembered that violence occurred on only a handful of campuses. However, the headlines of Harvard, Cornell, Berkeley, and CCNY had their impact on campus communities across the country. The caravans of television camera crews, the radio cars of the newspapermen, and the swarms of photographers made every college campus a source of news. Reporters, looking for the "local angle," searched for every gathering of students as a possible riot. Newsmen made the campus a "beat," interviewing at first amused and later annoyed college students on every aspect of their disenchantment with university life.

The final dismay came from students who were themselves interviewed—and misquoted, or at least misinterpreted.

"Yes, I was interviewed by the local reporter. He talked to me for about ten minutes. He seemed like a nice guy," said a Pennsylvania student. "Then, sure enough, he ran the story the next day. He used my name and everything and completely misquoted me."

The radical students are jubilant beyond measure at the

success they have achieved through publicity. It is probably fair to state that such success has bred daring and determination. The press has been, at best, used to bringing presidents to their knees and universities to a halt. This is neither the wish nor the machination of the overall college generation. To most students, it is the teamwork of the media and the radicals. It has not helped to promote meaningful dialogue.

Newspapers and magazines have been eager to print letters taken from official files. Hundreds of reporters were present at Cambridge during the Harvard turmoil, which was reported in detail; yet on hundreds of other campuses, quiet, unreported meetings among faculty, administrators, and student representatives have created and brought about changes in the university life that will continue. At Princeton, where television spent thousands of dollars to cover a riot that unfortunately, for them, failed to materialize, student-trustee meetings are bringing about many changes in campus life. At Amherst, a two-day session, with the whole school participating in a forum, covered every aspect of university life, and was, in the opinion of the whole campus, a great step forward. Yet the *New York Times* coverage was a page-one reference to a letter that Amherst's president sent to President Nixon calling for an awareness of social reform as the students' real aims. Amherst students were incensed at the failure to set forth the real constructive purpose of the forum.

To the great majority of college people, campus reforms are a family affair. Many believe news media should be banned from the campus. Students want to call a halt to the television and news coverage of student meetings. They expect editors and network officials to exercise greater judgment and restraint in being used by radicals for publicity that creates false impressions of the campus scene as it really is. They trust that editors will not force officials and politicians, as well as educators, into ill-conceived "statements," lest they be considered unresponsive to the danger of campus revolts. And in the case of the blacks, the current publicity will, in the opinion of most students, only accentuate the separation of the races.

Students are aware that the editorials and broad press coverage have taken a high toll. They fear repressive measures on state and local levels that could set back the student movement. Students are aware that the public is concerned about the campus riots and oppression would give the radicals a new issue to exploit.

Most of all, students are bewildered by the publicity and wish the notoriety would go away. They are anxious to be left alone, to be taken off the front pages so they can continue a dialogue that has at last started.

If it can continue out of the limelight and if the radicals are brought under control, the chances of campus peace will be greatly improved, the College Poll shows.

Students expect the right to protest, within the law; and in turn, they expect that college authorities will enforce the laws against radicals. As more student participation takes place and communication lines open, the confrontation era may soon run its course.

CHAPTER SIX

The College Student
and Drugs

If one area of misunderstanding between the public and
student attitudes could be termed as typical of the generation gap, it might well be the subject of drugs on and off
campus.

Publicity given to college dope or drug raids, "LSD," and
the campus-hippie trip activities would give the impression
that this is a generation of drug addicts, and that colleges are
a haven for pushers and flower children who infest the
dormitories of the country. An alumni magazine recently
claimed that "if we could eliminate drug use on our campus,
most of the problems would be easily solved."

This statement reflects little actual understanding either of
the scope or of the nature of the campus drug problem.

First of all, what are the facts? How many students
actually use drugs of any kind? The figures are formidable
enough without embellishment or distortion.

The College Poll interviewers asked students on eighty-
seven campuses across the country, representing a cross section of the nation's full-time college population, this question:
"Have you ever taken drugs, such as marijuana or LSD?"
Thirty-eight percent answered yes, and 62 percent said no.

Considering that 38 percent of the full-time student body

represents about 2,500,000 students, the incidence of drug use is widespread indeed. In plain terms, the chances that a student entering college will eventually try drugs of some type is about two in five—a compelling figure.

This study makes no effort to determine the incidence of addiction. The purpose of the College Poll is to determine student opinions and attitudes, not their medical histories. But what the students do, in fact, think about drugs and drug-taking is relevant to the entire handling of the drug problem, and parental and college administration understanding of how to cope with it. For the drug problem is, to most students, another instance of the refusal by the older generation or Establishment "to tell it as it is," and another example of the imposition of unrealistic rules and regulations.

In an even broader sense, the college, parental, and official view of drugs represent to the college student—whether he in fact takes drugs or not—another evidence of "dishonesty" on the part of the older generation and a glaring instance of its failure to realize that the college generation has reached maturity.

Such broad conclusions are not gathered from the mere statistics or summaries of student attitudes, but rather from an examination of the comments and reasons given by the students themselves in personal, in-depth interviews with the College Poll representatives.

The study reveals many interesting basic trends about drug use by students. For example, college men are more likely to try drugs than coeds. The chances are that freshmen are least likely to try drugs—with sophomores the most likely. And the study reveals that more and more students are trying drugs before they come to college.

First of all, it is important to identify what we mean by drug usage. When collegians speak of having tried drugs, by and large they mean marijuana, or pot or grass, as it is interchangeably known. It appears that most have tried it first either at a party or with a roommate or friend. Normally, it is not a drug initially tried alone. Most have tried it off campus and not in a dormitory, according to the College Poll interviewers.

Why did they try it? In most instances, they did it for "kicks" or on a "dare," or because they were just plain "curious." Rarely did they take it originally from a stranger or a "pusher." And it appears that at the time they took it they were "ready for it," either because of trouble with marks, or a date, or as part of an "in-between" period, or "on the rebound." The first attempt was almost always casual as to time, and not planned at any particular place.

What did they think of it? Almost all were disappointed.

"There was hardly any kick or sensation," said a Purdue sophomore.

"It was a washout," added a Marietta junior.

"Well, it was sort of interesting, but it was completely different from what I expected," said a Goucher senior.

"Like kissing sister," said a Stanford junior, laconically. "But this attitude changes after continued usage."

How widespread is the use? In addition to the large numbers who have tried it, the use is widely distributed. Its availability is quite universal on the campus, particularly in large urban colleges and universities all across the country.

"You can get pot anywhere on campus," declared a Penn junior.

"There's usually someone with a joint at every party," said a Chicago U. sophomore. (A joint is a frequently used cigarette containing marijuana and sold singly.)

Many campuses have "freak-out" rooms located nearby where students can go to smoke marijuana. Students can buy marijuana either on or off campus, and prices are rather stabilized because the supply is so ample, the College Poll representatives were told.

Students cite fellow students, local citizens, and even young professors as sources of supply. In some places, students even grow their own marijuana, although the danger of being caught that way is thought to be greater than buying it as needed. Student pushers of marijuana seem to be accepted as social equals, with none of the moral stigma motion pictures usually attribute to "dope peddlers." Few students actually know where it comes from originally, but some mention Mexico, or the West Coast. But wherever it comes from, it's accessible with care on almost every American campus, large or small, urban or rural.

Were they worried about taking it? Most students said no. The key fact is that students don't believe that taking marijuana is dangerous to their health.

When the College Poll asked the students, "Do you believe that marijuana is dangerous to your health?", 62 percent said no, 32 percent said yes, and 6 percent said they were not sure, or had no opinion.

It's this deep-seated conviction that marijuana is not harmful that encourages students to try it, with little sense of concern, guilt, or consequence.

"There's no evidence that marijuana is any more dangerous than smoking cigarettes," said a Trinity sophomore. "In fact, it's probably less harmful."

"I'd never have tried pot if I thought it was dangerous," explained a Colorado freshman. "In fact, I don't believe this nonsense about the weed being harmful."

"The research that has been done proves marijuana is not dangerous," a Georgia Tech senior stated categorically.

"If it were true that marijuana is harmful, there would be plenty of studies put out by the government, like those against cigarettes" was the opinion of a Louisiana State biology major.

Of equal importance is that students completely reject the argument advanced by parents and authorities for shunning marijuana—fear of addiction.

"There's no evidence that marijuana causes addiction" was the statement of an Illinois freshman. "In fact, medical testimony says it is not habit-forming at all."

Since it is not dangerous and not addictive, students feel little moral stigma to taking marijuana. "My parents naturally don't want me to smoke marijuana. Actually, I didn't like it after I tried it. I didn't get much of a kick out of it, but I don't feel as if I committed a crime or a sin. After all, there's really no harm in it," said a Vassar sophomore in a typical statement.

Students most frequently quote two sources for their opinions about marijuana. A few years ago, Dr. James Goddard, the head of the Food and Drug Administration, stated that marijuana was no more harmful than alcohol or a cigarette. It will probably rank as one of the most quoted government-official statements of all time. Students also state that their professors admit that marijuana is a nondangerous drug.

But even more frequently mentioned is the campaign conducted by *Playboy*, a frequently read publication on the campus. The magazine has maintained a steady editorial policy against existing laws outlawing marijuana, with arguments often cited by students in interviews on the campus.

"Read *Playboy*," said an NYU sophomore. "Every month they have authorities who say that marijuana is harmless."

As a Kent State junior put it. "Hugh Hefner has proved that marijuana is a harmless herb."

The seeming inconsistencies between school rules, state laws, and medical or scientific facts as students see them are the source of growing resentment by many students.

"Why don't they make laws based on truth? These marijuana laws were made long before there was any real scientific study of the drug. Marijuana is harmless, yet if I get caught with it in this state, I not only get thrown out of school, I could get a year in jail," said a Sante Fe sophomore. "It's a farce." (New Mexico's antidrug laws are particularly severe.)

"The school rules about marijuana are just as phony as many of the other regulations here," said a St. Louis University junior. "One professor admitted to us that there was no real proof that marijuana is dangerous; yet they'd bounce us out on this rap without a second thought. It's completely dishonest."

Less direct but of equal conviction is the feeling of many students that the laws should at least differentiate between harmless and harmful drugs—and between addicts and occasional users. In this connection, many student papers are taking up the subject of reform of drug laws.

The students' attitude should be of concern also to parents preoccupied with a widening relationship or credibility gap with their college sons and daughters.

"My father still says that pot is bad, but he knows he has no proof," said a Virginia sophomore. "He just won't admit he's wrong, because he wants to back up the school. That's no way to build confidence."

A Smith junior describes a discussion with her family. "I don't always agree with my parents, anyway. But when they write me they'll pull me out of school if I try smoking marijuana, I blow up."

"It's not for real. My parents really know better," commented an Immaculata junior. "Not that I ever tried any drug. They just want me to take this on faith. If it's a matter of faith, that's one thing. But marijuana is a matter of scientific study—not faith."

Some students are less objective. "When parents say marijuana is bad for you, it's just another example of the older generation not knowing the facts," said a Miami junior.

Student attitudes on the harmlessness of marijuana take on other shades of meaning as well. We have seen that most believe marijuana is harmless to themselves either as a health or addictive measure. Others defend it as harmless to society —an "innocent social drug."

"What harm does it do to let a man take marijuana?" asked a Hamilton sophomore. "He does no harm to himself. But more important, he does no harm to society. Alcohol often turns a man into a swinging drunk, who will either hurt his companions, or smash his car into a tree. But marijuana is a quiet drug that enables one to contemplate or have deeper personal introspection. That is not only not bad, it is even good."

But if students have a liberal view toward marijuana, College Poll interviews show just the opposite about LSD, which has received much more off-campus publicity. Significantly, the real reason for limited use of LSD by students, in the face of marijuana use, is the belief that LSD is a dangerous drug and marijuana is not.

For example, most students when asked, "Is LSD harmful to your health?", responded as follows: Seventy-six percent said yes, 12 percent said no, and 12 percent were either not sure or had no opinion. The result is that students refrain, for the most part, from taking LSD or any of the hallucinogenic drugs.

The same is true of heroin. Not one student interviewed had taken or even tried heroin.

"You think I'm crazy! That's a sure way to get hooked," said a Fordham senior. Even a Berkeley student, described by the College Poll interviewer as a hippie, said, "I may be far out, but I'm not crazy enough to take that stuff."

"LSD would affect the health of my children," said a Vassar sophomore. "I wouldn't take a chance like that."

"LSD can hurt your mind," declared a Fordham junior. "That's not worth any short-term advantage in a trip."

A Michigan State freshmen said, "Few of my classmates have ever taken LSD—it's too scary. However, we've tried pot a lot."

"A friend of mine took LSD last year, just once," reported a Tulane sophomore. "He got all mixed up and dropped out."

Such word-of-mouth rejection of LSD helps restrict use and overcome temptation to gamble on a "tryout trip" or "first flight."

It seems the use of hallucinogenic drugs is generally

limited to the hippie element on campus, whereas grass or pot, has attained a certain social status, similar to that enjoyed by liquor or even cigarettes. LSD is a "far-out" drug, unacceptable to most students at parties or fraternity or sorority houses.

"We don't allow any acid freaks in this place," said an Ohio Wesleyan fraternity member.

"Those guys [users of LSD] are bad news," said a Yale secret-society leader. "We spot them fast and keep them out."

While this mature attitude toward LSD represents the majority view, there is a liberal element on campus who takes a different view. In answer to the charge that LSD and hallucination trips are useless and harmful, a Notre Dame senior said, "Who can claim that these drugs are useless? They open new vistas for the mind and new channels for creativity and thought. Take music, for example. John Lennon, the Beatle, was writing 'Yeah! Yeah! Yeah!' before he went on drugs, His recent music, drug induced, is classic. Much creative thought of today may well come from drug-induced new avenues of mental exploration and creativity."

Among the intellectual and more introspective campus students, the College Poll reports the use of hallucinogenic drugs defended as "enlarging concepts and ideas"; "extending human experience"; and "a method of mental stimulation that opens new vistas, as psychiatry did for the spirit." But even among these, actual use seems limited.

Despite publicity about campus sex and drugs, there appears to be little verification of its interrelations as far as most students are concerned. While a few students, particularly at the large urban universities, admit hearing of sex and drug orgies on or near the campus, not one student admitted to the poll as ever having participated in such an affair.

On the other hand, as a University of California junior put it, "Those hippies who live off campus may be doing anything. And whatever they do they usually have a photographer or newsreel man around taking pictures of it. Then people believe we're all like that."

In addition to marijuana and LSD, the College Poll reveals that some students take a drug known as "speed." Speed comes under the general heading of drugs referred to as the amphetamines, of which the most common varieties are benzedrine and dexedrine. Usually dispensed in the form of women's diet pills, the drugs can be procured with relative ease near almost any campus.

Law-enforcement authorities and parents are considerably worried about the speed scene that has seen many hippie youths and some of the more daring teen-agers from suburban areas take heavy dosages of amphetamines in order to keep going on wild weekends. Others have even progressed beyond the pill stage to fast-acting methedrine, sold in crystalline form in small envelopes, and taken in much the same way as heroin.

However, the College Poll interviewers in their survey of the drug scene on America's campuses found little or no evidence of the use of methedrine in powdered form by students. Those students who use speed limit themselves to pills that they take in order to stay awake in preparing for examinations or to fight fatigue while traveling. However, some undergraduates did admit that, if they want to be sure not to miss any fun during weekend trips, they will occasionally resort to speed.

Typical comments from student users of speed are as follows:

"I can stay awake and study better after I've had speed," said a Miami University sophomore.

"Speed not only helps me stay awake—I can retain facts better," reported a Penn junior.

Other students claim these drugs help them in taking exams. "I seem sharper and less nervous when I've taken some before the exams," said a Washington State junior.

"I can prove I've done better with them on exams," stated a Norwalk College freshman.

These are "personal" as opposed to "social" drugs and, although quite widely used at college, are rarely publicized or discussed on campus, College Poll interviewers indicate.

With all the discussion as to the widespread drug usage, it is easy to forget that the majority of students do not use—in fact, have not tried—drugs of any kind. If 38 percent of the students admit taking drugs, 62 percent say they have not—a total of 4,500,000 college students who reject drugs absolutely at this stage of their careers.

For those who would make drug use legal, college student opinion is a powerful argument in the negative. Students who do not use, or have not tried, drugs consider legal sanction as the principal reason for abstaining, the College Poll shows.

"One slip and your career is over," said a Columbia sophomore. "One of these days the law is going to make an example of some student, and I don't want it to be me."

"No matter how you put it, taking and selling drugs is illegal," said a Sante Fe sophomore. "It's not worth it for a kick, even if it's wrong to have the laws as they are."

In addition, there is some evidence of a student "backlash" against campus drug use. Many students resent the image created on their campuses by drug users. Although ordinarily tolerant of student preferences, some students are fearful of public action on their campuses due to drug-taking.

A sophomore at Stony Brook College (a Long Island, New York, college that has been a regular target for police drug raids) expressed this view well.

"This college has a bad name merely because a few students got mixed up with drugs. Most of them will be dropouts anyway. I want to transfer to a four-year school and I can tell I'm going to have a tough time."

Other students see a different and ominous danger in the

widespread drug-use situation itself. Most colleges have student courts or student codes that outlaw drugs of any kind on campus. While some student courts do take action, most are reluctant to do so.

"You really can't accuse a student of a crime, which is what drug-taking really is, without arousing the whole student body," said a student officer.

As a Georgetown University junior put it, "All we need now is a student riot over drugs. The activists know that this would be a real issue. Just let the university single out one of these acid freaks and they [the activists] would tear the whole university apart."

As for university officials, they appear to be following a hands-off attitude for the most part. Beyond lending their moral and official sanction against all drug use, college officials tend to leave law enforcement up to local authorities, the College Poll survey shows. Most drug experiences occur off campus, in any event, but where police or governmental authorities become involved, college officials cooperate as in any law-enforcement matter. Nevertheless college authorities are clearly worried by the drug situation.

An Illinois college officer summarized the problem as follows:

"It's another case of a lack of real authority over the student. Students are leading much more independent lives than ever before. Since they don't feel drug-taking—marijuana in particular, is dangerous—they are, in effect, breaking the law continuously. Our problem is one of education and reaching the student with a new approach to the dangers of addiction. While isolated drug-taking may be harmless, the real danger, that of developing psychological substitutes, and increasing reliance on such substitutes with more demanding reaction, is lost on most students. Their argument is as specious as the claim, 'One cigarette does not make cancer.' We are also aware that a whole new generation of synthetic drugs will be available in the near future. This creates an educational problem of increasing importance."

In sum and substance, then, the College Poll shows a significant percentage of drug users (2,500,000) on America's campuses. And the problem is compounded by ample evidence that the smoking of marijuana or pot is increasing. Many students are obviously breaking the law regularly, in many cases unwittingly, and thereby risk the incurrence of penalties that could ruin their careers before they get started. Moreover, as one college police official stated:

"As these colleges get larger, the business gets bigger and that attracts the hoodlums, presenting a constant threat to the academic community."

The encouraging fact is that if, as with LSD, students can be convinced that a drug is dangerous, its use will be drastically curtailed. It must also be remembered that there are 4,500,000 students who have not and do not use drugs—an affirmative force on the campus for the restriction of drug use. However, the poll clearly demonstrates that little impact will be made upon any student by presenting arguments that don't "tell it as it is."

CHAPTER SEVEN

Students Flunk
the Faculty

The traditional view of a college professor is that of a benign, learned, interested purveyor of knowledge and wisdom, attended by a dedicated, mesmerized, adoring class. It's a myth. Mr. Chips is really dead.

If students had their choice on only one element in which they would improve their college or university, it wouldn't be more student power or better food or even greater social freedom. The College Poll study on what students really want puts better teachers as the first area for improvement.

When asked the question by College Poll interviewers: "In what ways would you bring about improvement in your school?", 46 percent of all students placed better teachers as the number-one demand.

Yet, dissent makes strange bedfellows. You rarely see signs against the faculty in newspapers or television coverage of student riots. In fact, paradoxically enough, members of the faculty themselves may be in line protesting against the Establishment.

Students are deeply concerned about their teachers. They go to college to learn and to pass subjects. They expect the teacher to be proficient in his subject and able to present it with competence and interest. Too often they are disappointed, and it is this concern about the level of teaching that is a constant source of irritation on·the campus.

Not that there aren't many fine, dedicated professors and instructors at all levels. But there aren't enough of them, and this, in turn, makes students concerned about the quality of their education. It starts with the concept of what a faculty is for, and to most students it's quite simple—to teach.

"I expect a professor to be able to teach me a subject," said a Vanderbilt junior. "I don't care about his professional academic background, his degrees, or whether or not he's the head of a department. He's there to get me through a course, and half the time I know he doesn't care whether I make it or not."

Students believe that professors should be rated for their classroom effectiveness and not for their academic degrees.

"We are arguing that professors should be selected for how well they teach and not on the basis of how much research he has done," commented a Tufts junior. "My best teacher last year was one who didn't want to do research—he wanted to teach. The university put pressure on him and now he's gone."

"We know better than the trustees whether or not a professor is paying off in class. We should be able to rate them on their ability. The administration never listens to them in class," said an Ohio Wesleyan sophomore. "But after a few years, these professors get tenure and future students are stuck with them."

Students on many campuses have set up rating services in which teachers are evaluated. The Louisiana State Student Council publishes a book about the campus faculty and evaluates each professor on personality and teaching ability. The Harvard student publication does this regularly. Several fraternities put out rating sheets on teachers and courses. The comments are frank and often helpful. In some cases they are brutal. But it does reflect the fact that students are serious about the men and women who run the courses they have to pass. A great number worked hard to get to college, and have to work harder to stay in. To most students, professors are not entitled to respect just because of their degrees or scholarships. The real test takes place in the classroom. The professional nature of the college professor is not generally recognized by students. While not exactly employees, teachers are considered by students as a means to an end—and are well paid for their work. On balance, the entire student body feels the quality of teaching is low.

On the other hand, men and women who attend graduate schools, business courses, or professional schools seem more satisfied with their professors.

"In Accounting, our professor is a real pro. He worked for a firm before he came back to teach and he knows his stuff," said a Penn business administration major.

A Marquette economics major explained, "When professors have been out in the world, they are more practical and know what's important and what isn't. Our economics teacher is a banker, and he makes things realistic."

A Dartmouth graduate student summed up the opinion of many. "There is a maturity that comes in graduate work. Teachers know what you are after, and you know what is expected of you. In college, you expect more guidance from your professors, and usually you don't get it."

The lack of accessibility of students to professors irks many collegians. If students put better teachers as the number-one complaint, the second is "closer student-teacher relationships" in the College Poll study. When one realizes that the lack of personal relationships is one of the key faults of our society in the minds of students, the inaccessibility of the teacher is another indication that the university has, indeed, become an impersonal institution— typical of the Establishment that the student wishes to change or avoid. The teacher is the real day-by-day contact with the student. More than the dean, or the president or the trustee, the teacher or professor is "Mr. Education"—the personification of the teaching process. Lack of dialogue here can be frustrating and, in terms of the student's own performance, a fatal blow to his education. Not all teachers are inaccessible. Many give generously of their time and interest. But the odds against the student-teacher relationship that provides encouragement and understanding are, indeed, getting greater.

With class enrollment totaling as high as one thousand at times, students have no feeling of empathy with their teachers—and vice versa. In larger schools, television presentations are used, creating an even more impersonal atmosphere. In forum classes, students frequently complain that they can't hear the professor. Classes become routine "note-taking sessions," with professors seemingly bored with their classes and disinterested in their subjects. Even in smaller schools, students object to faculty unavailability.

"Professors are either writing a book, or on a lecture tour for some corporation," said a Duke junior. While probably exaggerated, many professors are, indeed, tied up with outside work, or doing research for papers.

This complaint about levels of teacher proficiency is evidenced in schools of all levels, male and female, city and rural alike.

Students are not always aware of the problems. While the pay of professors has risen in recent years, it still is not high enough to compete with industry standards. The university is fighting for talent in a shrinking labor market, and the best talent is not always willing to make the sacrifice to stay on campus. And there are hardly enough teachers of any quality to man the growing staff of the expanding number of colleges.

Moreover, the faculty itself is in a state of tension with the university and college administration—a situation often reflected in student-teacher relations. With high priority on research and scholarship, good teachers are in a sellers' market and move from campus to campus. Many West Coast schools, like Berkeley, for example, are losing some of their top professors to Eastern schools for reasons which some say are political and others claim are monetary.

The sight of teachers striking and bargaining collectively may be necessary for economic survival, but it does not aid the teachers' image in student eyes. Students particularly resent tenure—the perpetuation of the mediocre—for which teachers strive at all costs. Many courses are taught by graduate assistants, just a few years older than students themselves and lacking in authority or experience.

Students also resent the unevenness of marking by teachers. Disagreement with marking procedures is fairly universal.

When asked, "Is the present system of grade marking in your school satisfactory?", 54 percent of all students said no.

The younger students are more likely to object to marking systems than are seniors or graduate students. Schools have done much to study the marking systems. The "pass-fail" system has been tried in some colleges. Under this program, students may take a course with only one choice of a mark —"pass or fail." If he fails, the marks do not appear on the school record. If he passes, the word "pass" is on his record. The system was set up primarily to encourage students to take courses for their own interest, without regard to marks. Thus, if the course was too difficult, a failure would not appear on the record. But the fear of failure would not prevent the student from taking the course.

This program has been received with mixed reaction. It is objected to mostly by students intending to go on to graduate school who customarily state that a mere "pass" mark doesn't help them in winning acceptance to the higher educational institutions. Yet it remains one of the many innovations schools are installing to meet student demands for a better marking system. But, in the last analysis, it is not so much the "system" as it is the men and women professors who determine the marks that bother students.

There are no objective standards to the marking process. In fact, many students accuse teachers of varying their grades often on caprice and whim. This infuriates students who, in many cases, take courses with professors who are known to mark easier, in preference to courses they would elect under other circumstances. The students have no more respect for the "easy marker," but they resent bad marks from professors who have no contact with them, or evaluate a whole semester on the basis of one or two papers. While the whole area of marks and grades is necessarily subjective, the campus consensus is that the strict mark does not necessarily mean the teacher is good or that he demands much from his students.

"There is no appeal from a bad mark," said a Florida State sophomore. "And generally it's the worst prof who lays the goose eggs."

But if the size and quality of the faculty are the main issues, the whole subject of curriculum is the next most important to students. The College Poll shows that few riots ever occur because of curriculum reform (except the demand for Afro-American studies), but it is one of the deeper resentments of students for all levels of academic achievement that enables less popular issues to be exploited by activists into an overall dissatisfaction with school officials.

There are several basic complaints about the college curriculum. The first is that it is too rigid. It should be pointed out that the curriculum has always been a bone of contention between students and professors, between professors and deans, and sometimes between deans and trustees. The current curriculum is an evolvement of many compromises coming in part out of Germany decades ago, reviewed and reformed by such educators as Dr. Eliot of Harvard, and debated by educators ever since. The purpose of the curriculum is to provide a student with an education by selecting certain areas of study that will give him specific knowledge in a field of his interest or choice—and hopefully, a balanced view of overall knowledge in other fields to make him truly an educated gentleman.

It's the balances that cause the problems with educators. As the emphasis in recent years has shifted toward specialization in life, educators have, in turn, been forced to make the curriculum more specific. Industry, arts, education, and science all require greater training to fulfill job specifications. Thus it has not been an easy task for educators to keep up, not only with the change in curriculum requirements for specialization, but also the great variety of new disciplines our new society has created. Not only must new studies be created, but new facilities developed, and new teachers trained. Growth within certain specific fields has been huge. For example, the physics book of 1969 is four times the size of the physics text of 1949.

The practical result has been to force the student to specialize—to select a routine of study at an early age of his college career. It is not easy to transfer from one integrated course to another. Schedules of classes are crowded, and courses are filled up quickly. In larger universities, course selection is by computer. A California student gets a printout of his courses—like reserving an airline ticket. In smaller schools, a "first come, first served" procedure has to apply. Few parents are aware of these problems of scheduling and selecting courses. But it does affect students deeply and since their lives are shaped at this time, it creates much bitterness and disillusionment.

Students thus feel, even in the early years of their education, that they are being forced to conform to rules of a society with which they are not sure they agree. The educational process seems to be restricted to "fitting into a slot"— not enlarging the horizons. And even the liberal-arts courses appear, to most students, ill designed to acquaint students with knowledge that will fit into their evaluation of the world.

For example, if a student is to receive a degree in humanities, he is required to take certain courses that are of no essential interest to him, and are based upon arbitrary and archaic criteria of what a humanities degree should mean. The humanities of 1969 are not even the humanities of 1959.

"The catalog says we are being trained to be mature and developed citizens—well rounded to face life's responsibilities," said an Illinois junior. "My required courses don't accomplish that. I'm more a historian."

"There are a lot of courses I want to take but can't," said a Goucher senior, bitterly. "Now that I'm almost through school, I feel I could have spent my time to much better advantage studying subjects other than those I was required to take."

"There's no reason in the world why I should be required to take a foreign language," a Southern Methodist sophomore said. "I never liked it, I hated it in high school, and I'm not doing well at it now. The catalog said it is necessary. You tell me why. There are so many other ways I could use the time and effort."

"When I finished my second year, I decided I wanted to go into nursing. They told me I'd have to start all over, even though I could have filled in the hours on other relevant courses," said a coed at Ladycliff. "It wasn't the science courses, it was the liberal-arts courses because that was what the degree required. It's nonsense."

These attitudes are typical. In studying a college catalog it will be seen that degree requirements are quite strict. To an incoming freshman, they are a maze. It may not be until a year later that he discovers he is prevented from switching from one course to another as his ideas about his life change.

"When you come to college you don't really know what you want. Some guys are lucky. Their father is a lawyer and they want to be a lawyer. Or some girl wants to study archaeology. That's fine," commented a Purdue sophomore. "But when I came here I thought I wanted to be an engineer, and now I'm not sure. But if I switch now it will take another year or more to get a degree in anything but engineering. There should be another way."

In addition to objecting to rigidity, students want at least some of their courses to be more relevant. A frequently misunderstood word, "relevant" to most students means that it relates to something he knows, experiences, or will experience in his life. It helps prepare him to take his place in the world as he sees it.

"I spent last year in History III, a course covering ancient civilization where I had to memorize ten thousand dates and names," said a Kansas City sophomore. "I can't remember one now, although I got a B. But why not some more relevant course? I had to take it to graduate. I would rather have taken a course on urban problems."

"Why must we take these rigid courses that leave no real choice to the student?" asked a Wisconsin junior. "These courses I'm taking are all right for the guy who wants to be an economist, but they don't help me learn about society and how to solve the problems we have to face as human beings."

"College wasn't meant just to learn a trade," commented a Michigan State sophomore. "Yet I feel everything I'm learning is merely an extension of some specialized training—not a learning process. What's more, I've never had a chance to ask any professor a simple question in class since I've been in school."

"I believe the school catalog was made up in 1853, the year the school was founded," observed a Manhattan College senior. "They have made a lot of progress, but we still study traditional courses in traditional form. I find myself educated to defend the past—not inspire the future."

It is not all negative, however. Students who hold teachers in contempt for poor performance are loyal almost to a fault in crediting individual excellence among faculty members. In at least a dozen institutions this year, students protested the dismissal of a professor who rated well by student standards, but fell short by administration evaluation. Students praise openly a professor who teaches a course, who marks fairly, and who shows an interest in students, their questions, their aims, and their futures. Students flock to newer courses that have interest and relevancy for them. Actually, most students really want greater latitude, not free or complete control over the subjects—which many outsiders believe are student goals.

Much credit also goes to guidance counselors, faculty advisers, and professors who try hard to resolve student course and class conflicts. They help many a despairing student at a critical time of his career.

Student demands to rate teachers on classroom performance, mastery of subject, fairness of grading, and other key measurements have met with dismay on the campus. College authorities properly assert that students may not be the best judge of a professor's worth to the institution. The authorities claim that only other professors can rate the value of his publication, how well he serves on and contributes to faculty committees, and how much he is worth to the profession or discipline he serves. These factors may be the province of the university and even the professors themselves.

The university may also be happy to have *any* teacher to fill the expanding number of courses catalogs contain. Hard pressed to find men and women with appropriate collegiate backgrounds, the university and college have frequently had to cancel courses for lack of supervision.

"Imagine a Mark Rudd running our faculty evaluation meetings," said a Columbia professor, who chilled at the prospect.

"Excellence is unfortunately a quality lacking on both sides of the desk," commented an Ivy League dean, dryly.

Students themselves do not have the answers. Many attempt to set up their own relevant courses, often with school approval. The University of Colorado has its underground courses, at which university professors teach, gratis. Michigan State, Stanford, Syracuse, Harvard, and others maintain outside courses, held in dormitories or off campus, to solve the demand for relevance. Some of the courses bear such titles as "Rebellion Good or Bad," and "The Negro." And at Davidson, a course in pornography is now offered.

The best hope is for students to be heard directly in connection with curriculum reform and teacher evaluation. Accordingly, more and more schools have admitted students to faculty and administration boards to encourage curriculum reform and faculty review.

Many educators feel the student membership is welcome at an advisory level. Some faculty members have encouraged student participation in administrative and policy discussions, if not decisions, of this nature. In fact, responsible students do not expect more than an advisory role. The transient nature of a study body militates against its ability to function adequately in the area of long-term commitments of responsibility and judgment. Change in so basic an area as a curriculum is difficult to accomplish quickly. Many colleges have long-range plans in this direction that have not been adequately delineated to students. Some newly founded groups have been surprised to discover at joint meetings with authorities that their university has been planning changes in grading and curriculum more advanced than student imagination had conceived.

There is a reason for the insistence and immediacy of student complaints about teachers and curriculum that is often overlooked. Students are willing to listen and discuss specific proposals at some length. In fact, they are more than likely to admit that the non-negotiating president is as rare as the non-negotiating student.

But to the argument that the "university is working on it" or "we have such plans under advisement," the answer is that this is a "now" generation that feels that slow change may be no change at all insofar as it is concerned. Red tape, lengthy plans, long deliberations, and debate are part of the Establishment and the impersonality of the era that students reject.

"I'm only going to be here for two more years. I'm not too interested in building a new monument called 'New Curriculum' for myself. I want to get something out of my four years here," said a Columbia senior.

"I feel I'm wasting my time in college—and I only have one crack at it," is the attitude of a Madison Wisconsin freshman.

"My mother and father keep telling me I should be grateful I'm in college," commented a Tennessee sophomore. "But if I'm not getting what I should out of it, who am I really fooling—my parents or myself?"

"The dean will be here for another twenty years. He looks at us like this year's wheat crop," commented an MIT junior. "We're not a crop, we're people, and we should be dealt with now as individuals. Don't use us to improve the grain over the years."

Not all student demands are practical economically or desirable academically in the area of faculty evaluation or curriculum reform. Nevertheless, students feel they are not getting their money's worth. They desire other values for measurement of teaching performance than mere scholarship, and a reevaluation of curriculum from traditional guidelines of academic achievement, created for an era that has passed, and ill designed to educate students for today's world.

It's a viewpoint everyone should preserve—students, faculty, and the administration alike, if the student dissension is to be useful and productive.

CHAPTER EIGHT

Is God Dead?

God is not dead on the campus. But the chapels are empty.

That simple statement sums up the dilemma surrounding religion on the campus. No, God is not dead at all among our college generation. Atheism is not running rife on our campuses. When students were asked the question—"Do you believe in God or a Supreme Being?", 73 percent answered yes, 19 percent said no, and 8 percent had doubts or didn't answer.

Yes, God is indeed quite alive in the hearts and minds of our university people—maybe even more than in the hearts of their parents.

Behind this seemingly simply analysis are overtones that explain, in part, the growing impasse between the church and college students.

Students have their own ideas about God—ideas that are much different from the stereotyped concepts of their parents or that were taught to them in Sunday school or parochial school.

There is no lack of reverence, however. To most students, God is indeed "a Supreme Being who controls life," as a Kansas State senior explained.

"God is a spirit—a spiritual force," said a North Carolina State freshman.

"God is a mystical being," a Boston University sophomore indicated.

"God is really not a person as we know a person to be," said a Brown freshman. "But He is real."

For a generation reluctant to take matters on faith, today's students readily rationalize the necessity of the existence of a Supreme Being.

"The order of the world demands the existence of a rational being who created it all," said a Penn State sophomore in an argument that might issue from any book on apologetics.

"The universe has to be the product of an intelligent being who put it together with reason and form," a Miami U. senior explained.

"I see God in a flower, in the ocean, in the symmetry of the forest and the stars," said a Smith College junior.

These comments are typical. God, the Supreme Being, the Creator of the universe, the moving Spirit of the world, is all quite real and acceptable to most students. The principal foundation of this belief is their ability to reason such an existence. Beyond that, it gets different and difficult.

"I don't necessarily believe in a God who punishes and sends you to hell."

"God is not the Almighty Being who sets right and wrong, and whose forgiveness you have to ask."

"God is not religion."

"God isn't going to church."

From these typical statements it is clear that most students differentiate clearly between God and religion. While they are perfectly willing to accept, through reason, the existence of a Supreme Being, no such reassuring process requires them to accept the tenets of religion or any formal manner of worshiping that Being.

"I can reason there is a God," said a Harvard sophomore. "But I can't reason I have to go to church."

When the College Poll asked the question—"Have you been to church services of any kind in the last seven days?", 36 percent said yes; 64 percent said no.

The traditional concept of worshiping in church, at formal ceremonies, with altars and pulpits and the ancestral hymns is completely unacceptable to most students. There is also a challenge to all formal religion, and a deep-seated question as to whether one needs a "minister of God" to guide and direct.

Not that they don't believe in worshiping a God. Students who see God everywhere feel they can worship Him anywhere.

"Worshiping God means recognizing Him as a Supreme Being and admiring His work," explained a University of California sophomore. "When I go to the ocean and see the waves and the beauty of the seaside, that is a reflection of God to me, and a form of worship."

Some students feel that God is nature, and that God is love. Acts of worship to them may be a nature walk.

"I hope to find God in my marriage. Two people dedicated to each other for life is the best way of loving God."

These concepts of individual worship are expressed in many different forms:

"I worship God by studying."

"One can worship God by merely acknowledging His existence."

"You don't need a crowd to worship God."

"God is music—it draws out one's soul."

Thus, there appears to be a growing devotion to God on the basis of personal experience.

These attitudes are not the expression of the hippies, the flower people, the mods. These thoughts represent all students—the conservative, the coed, the well-dressed driver of a Triumph or an Alfa Romeo as well as the bearded radical. The emphasis toward emotional and informal worship and movement away from the altar is a universal trend on the campus.

Coeds seem to attend church services more often than college males. But statistics reveal that the longer the student stays in college, the less he attends church or church services. Only 21 percent of seniors attend church, compared to 79 percent who do not.

Students who attend secular institutions are inclined to attend religious services more frequently. But churchgoing seems to decrease as time goes on, even in denominational schools. Schools have recognized that enforced religious attendance is unworkable. Many colleges, Catholic and Protestant alike, have dropped the requirement of Sunday or daily mass as a demand. Only a few schools with a deep religious commitment—like Brigham Young's Mormon ties— have regular required religious attendance. When left to their own choice, the students' churchgoing habits disappear rapidly.

To the churches then, the attitude of college students presents a real challenge. They appear to expect more from their church than hymn-singing, masses, or services. Becoming more involved in the times and problems of the day, they look almost universally to the church and its ministers for leadership or guidance in these areas, more than solace or a life in the "hereafter." Cynical though it may sound, it represents the basic areas where the lack of communication between church and the students really exists. Many students feel it is merely an extension of reevaluation of all of life's mature concepts, a seeking out of the meaning of basic truths on their own.

The Protestant attitude is best expressed by a Princeton senior. "Frankly, I find church services dull and old-fashioned. Most sermons are pretty bad and behind the times."

A Syracuse sociology major explained, "Most ministers just can't get to the real problem. They skirt all around the substantive issues and use platitudes as excuses. I leave church services feeling I have wasted my time."

The Princeton student is typical in many ways. Reared a Protestant, he went to private schools before entering Princeton. His parents were "religious," he explained, and attended church regularly. He was forced to attend Sunday school and church services at a private boarding academy. He believes in God, but not in the validity of the religious denomination of his family. He feels his church offers him little in the things he can relate to. He finds church services out of tune with the times and, therefore, simply doesn't attend.

He believes in God and some of the Commandments but feels it is his conscience that enforces them—not a minister or God. He believes in a life hereafter, but not necessarily in a Heaven or hell. He feels his denomination is hypocritical and that it is overcommitted to "foreign missions" while cities at home rot. He goes to church once in a while, often at the prodding of his family or his girl. He expects that he will not go to church more frequently when he gets out. He refuses to be called by any term other than "Christian," but feels even that has become a symbol of prejudice. He doesn't know the chaplain on the campus, and states there is no need for them to become acquainted.

Since religion and worship are a matter of reason to most of the students like the Princetonian, moral beliefs become a matter of conscience that do not require a minister, priest, or rabbi to guide or interpret them. Actually he is not alone. He is like most Protestants in Harvard, Michigan State, Stanford, and Occidental.

Marriage, divorce, taking the pill, stealing, and even sexual relations—in fact, all matters carrying moral overtones become a matter of one's conscience to most college students.

And it is not necessarily encouraging immorality, as many people believe.

Individual conscience is generally quite strict. Students are arriving at practically the same conclusions about the basic moral tenets of society, but generally by a different route. The big difference is that those areas of activity normally forbidden by church law or the dictates of a formalized religion are no longer honored or respected. Students stopped eating fish on Friday some years ago. Easter duty, and compulsory Sunday mass have been abandoned to all intents and purposes by many Catholic collegians. Protestants appear to take a similar view toward their religion. Like the Princetonian, many students feel, often unfairly, that religion is "hypocritical" and "dishonest" about its stand on the social and economic ills of the day.

"The churches talk about social justice and do nothing about it. Priests who take civil rights stands are disciplined," said Catholic students.

"The ministers preach about civil rights and morality but take no stand. My hometown church hasn't changed a bit to help Negroes in our town. My minister is still a WASP," said a Massachusetts Protestant junior.

The chaplains are equally the objects of a campus dilemma. Students like or dislike chaplains mostly as men, and not because of their religious affiliations. The chaplains themselves, faced with change within their own churches, are hard pressed to answer the piercing questions fired at them by students. Chaplains who cling to the "old religion" find themselves alienated from the mainstream of student life. Most chaplains are sincere, hard-working men of God, who find themselves the focal point of religious upheaval in an era of doubt.

Those religious advisers who agree with the new morality discover that they may make friends with students, but have little to offer by way of guidance or inspiring respect. On the reverse side of the coin, few students realize the difficulty of a chaplain's role. His stature on the campus has not improved with the rise of religious doubt. The most successful appear to be those who will not concede the invalidity of the tenets of their religion, but are willing to accept changes in the manner of worship.

Chaplains expressed this dilemma directly to College Poll interviewers. Since they live with students and observe them in their various moods, their views are important in assessing the status of religion on the campus. A Michigan campus chaplain expressed the attitude aptly when he said:

"We're faced with the problem of religion becoming secularized as opposed to remaining formalized. To many students church has become an instrument to effect change. When we explain that we only have moral persuasion to offer, students become apathetic. It's not unfair to state that some seem more concerned with the slums than their souls."

A Catholic chaplain in Washington stated another problem. "This is the era of 'now' with the students. They are more concerned with the here than the hereafter. They want miracles worked on cue, and in areas over which the church has little or no control. While we may disagree with their methods and deplore their rejection of all dogma, they have an instinct for good that we are trying hard to harness for effective action, not only for society but for their own salvation."

Another chaplain from a Southern college expressed this view: "The students' methodic doubt is merely a reflection of the times. The Catholic church has recognized the need for change in our own house. The mature student today has obvious, and in many cases justified, criticism of his church. We feel we are making headway in creating a more modern setting for the practice of worship. We may have started too late, but we're moving in the right direction. For all their seeming maturity, they are really mere boys and girls. They are seeking God with all their might. If they rely on reason alone, they will find disillusionment and despair. We have to restore faith to their lives—faith in God, faith in men, and faith in themselves."

Modernization, not abandonment, is a policy that seems to work. Students respect the efforts to modernize. Catholic students in general seem to accept the "new liturgy" as a trend.

"I went to mass this week for the first time this year," said a Villanova freshman. "It was a real folk mass and I could identify with the music. We all felt great after the mass, and we all sang. That's the best mass I ever attended." Similar remarks were made at Boston College, Trinity, Georgetown, and Santa Clara.

On the other hand, there are many students who believe the modernization of the mass is ludicrous. Raised strictly in accordance with the accepted, standard forms of traditional worship, these students from varying backgrounds have great difficulty adjusting to the new liturgy. According to their views, the willingness of the church to accept the folk mass is an expression of weakness that only adds to the bewilderment and disillusionment.

"The folk singer is a fad, and the folk mass is a fad," said a Marygrove senior. "Is the church going to change the liturgy to fit every fad that comes along?"

"I get disgusted when I go home and see my parents trying to get involved in folk masses," said a Creighton sophomore. "Folk music is almost dead now, and to see the sisters, priests, and old people trying to be 'in' is sad. It shows they really didn't believe in their religion at all."

While extreme, these opposing attitudes are shared by many. However, most students have taken the church's changes in stride.

Chaplains who recognize the students' concern for the social issues of the day find greater acceptance. Priests and ministers who help take part in solving social ills, particularly in areas around the school, are well received and respected. Many campus chaplains have cooperated and even led student drives to end housing bias and spearheaded slum aid programs and civil rights programs in towns around the schools, with the result that they have won the respect and admiration of the entire student body.

It is interesting to note, however, that students may reject their religion in many ways yet still wish to be classified. A Santa Clara student elaborated at great length on the falsehood of much of the dogma he had been taught "by rote" in parochial school. He agreed he did not attend mass regularly, rarely went to confession, did not own a rosary, ate meat on Friday (even before the Vatican Council edict), and did not believe in many of the commandments of the church. However, when he was asked to state his religion, he promptly answered, "Roman Catholic." Questioned again, he said he expected to be married by a Catholic priest, and be buried in Catholic grounds. He also expected to raise his children as Catholics, but when they were old enough he'd let them make up their own minds about their religion.

When questioned about the inconsistency of this position, he explained:

"The church will have been brought up to date by the time my children are old enough for school."

This ambivalence is evident not only among Catholics, but Episcopalians, Presbyterians, and Jews.

Jewish students, many of whom were raised during the Jewish dialogue between Reformed and Orthodox, are not generally active against religion on the campus. The bulk of them have already openly rejected the formal requirement of the Orthodox Jewish religion.

"It's impossible to live the life of an Orthodox Jew on campus, much less in society today," said a University of Syracuse political science major. "When I'm married I'll carry on the Jewish family life in principle, and I expect to be married by a rabbi and raise my family as Jews. But Orthodox Jewry is out as a way of life. The future of the Jews in America is assured only by learning to identify more closely with society as citizens, not exaggerating the differences with customs that add nothing to devotion or dedication. Jewry will have few Orthodox disciples from this college generation."

There is also a trend toward Ecumenism, the College Poll shows. Students are attending church services other than those of their own religion. Many Protestants are attending folk masses, often by open invitation. The trend is more dramatic among Catholics, who were long insulated against joint religious services and worship. Catholic Newman Clubs have conducted chaplain-led programs toward joint services and meetings all across the country.

Catholic students at Fairfield University attend Quaker meetings. Northern students attending Duke have attended Baptist meetings for the first time. Open discussions about religion and doctrines are definitely helping to promote understanding and to level religious differences. Class studies on religions of the world have helped create broader understanding among the various faiths.

With the downgrading of ceremony as the essence of religious service, the sermon has become the uppermost element of the church service in the minds of students.

Asked, "What do you pay most attention to at a religious ceremony?", 80 percent of all students cited the sermon. It has become the opportunity for dialogue between student and pastor. Too often it backfires. Sermons in the era of religious change are rarely direct or responsive enough to satisfy students' challenging minds. Question-and-answer sessions, largely conducted in Protestant services, have been effective in some cases. But all too often the presentation of traditional answers, appropriate in the seminary or presented by men raised in a different religious tradition, widens rather than bridges the gap.

Nor are church services always the appropriate place for a

question-and-answer period. Students who attend to ask questions come well informed and well prepared. A debate is generally fairest when the session is formal. Students want direct answers that are not easy to formulate and harder to express in a church atmosphere.

"They go for the jugular," complained a Midwestern minister.

"We get the same old dodge—God wills it," countered an Ohio State senior.

There is little doubt that the upheaval within the churches themselves has had its effect on collegiate respect for ecclesiastical authority. It must be remembered that students are particularly well informed, and read thoroughly all sides of subjects in which they are interested. It should also be remembered that criticism (constructive or otherwise) of authority is a priority of the day on campus. In this circumstance, our young men and women are quick to exploit weaknesses.

Students of this generation were raised in an atmosphere of ecclesiastical authority. The sight of well-meaning priests challenging their bishops, the questioning of established dogma of the church on matters of theology, birth control, celibacy, and scripture, to mention a few, have had this impact on college students. At the very least, all of this has not aided in building a strong foundation of churchgoing. Many younger priests and clergymen are chaplains, or graduate students on larger campuses. Being almost of the same age, they share many of the doubts about formal religion that frustrate undergraduates. Since they are able to communicate on a more equal level than the older chaplains, they unwittingly contribute to the confusion and doubt in the minds of many students. Priests on strike at Catholic university and St. John's, among others, have stimulated these doubts. Clergymen of all faiths have joined in demonstrations and, in a few isolated instances, in campus uprisings.

These participations, while welcome to some individuals, are disturbing to many students who have held traditionalist attitudes toward the clergy.

In summary, it would appear that the college student reflects in many ways the confusion of the times as far as religion is concerned.

—The college student believes in God or a Supreme Being, as the College Poll clearly indicates. In most cases, that belief has been self-determined, however.

—College men and, to a lesser extent, coeds desire to worship in their own way, rejecting in large measure the traditions of established church worship of any denomination.

—To the college generation, conscience and not church law or church precepts is the guidance force in human morality.

—The students reject religious practices, customs, and regulations that are arbitrary and not responsive to their current lives or are not essential to moral law or their own individual sanctity.

—Students are skeptical of religious leaders, principally because those leaders are not able to communicate to students with conviction and authority the real direction in which their lives should go. Students are also well aware of the doubts the religious themselves have as to the role of religion and its future course.

—In a position of transition, churches and ministers have placed too much emphasis on compromise in order to accede to student desires. The attempt by the church to "run with the students" has weakened the church in student eyes.

—Students see in their doubts not a rejection of God but a search for a more meaningful religious commitment that has a basic social awareness, and an honesty in evaluation toward truth that rejects the superficial and the hypocritical in religious practice.

—God is not dead—but the chapels are, indeed, empty on the campuses of America.

CHAPTER NINE

Business Fails the Campus Test

In a recent article in the *Wall Street Journal,* a business recruiter for one of America's leading corporations was quoted as saying, "Most students are interested in careers in industry and there is no prejudice against large corporations." He couldn't be more wrong.

Making money and getting ahead in a business career are not the main aims of America's college student. Today's college generation has an entirely different and less materialistic viewpoint toward life. Traditional puritan concepts of labor as an end in itself are all but rejected by the current generation.

Today's college student expects much more out of life than a good job, promotions, and pensions, personal interviews with College Poll interviewers reveal. In general terms, students have more respect for their talents and their lives than dedication to work in an impersonal atmosphere. They indicate a more individualistic approach to existence and their career potential. And they are particularly wary of being gobbled up by an organizational world, with its Orwellian labyrinth. The general tenor of the college class is against restraints of the industrialized complex that places premiums on conformity. Students want greater emphasis on human values. They expect that they will make a "contribution" of some sort. Thus they look for fulfillment in terms of their human potential, with less concentration on financial gains.

When asked the question, "Do you think you'd be happy working for a large corporation?", 54 percent of all students said, "No."

"A large corporation is much too competitive," declared a Penn State senior. "They put people against each other."

"There's no place for someone who wants to express himself in a large company" was the attitude of a Southern Methodist economics major. "If I go into business I'd like to go with a small company, or teach."

"A big company is run by cliques" was the opinion of a Tennessee senior. "My family was never 'in' with my father's company and consequently got no place."

"My father worked for a big company for twenty-three years," said a Northwestern sociology major. "He was fired on three weeks notice after the company changed hands. He gave his life to that company. He doesn't know anything else. Now he's working in a supermarket."

"I know I'll get ahead if the computer says so and in no other way," a Duke senior said emphatically.

It should be remembered, of course, that there is on the campus a group, constituting approximately 20 percent of the total school population, with a definite career in mind. These students are highly motivated, dedicated, hardworking semiprofessionals who are laboring toward set goals on a prescribed, and to them satisfactory, schedule. These are the accounting and economics majors who are well along toward B.S. degrees and probably graduate school for further study. Added to these are nursing majors, prelaw, medical, and dental students who are progressing toward a professional degree. There are others—statisticians, physicists, and the like who have a clear track to the future.

It is this group that is most likely to become candidates for the college recruiters from the large corporations in an annual draft, which has all of the drama but none of the publicity of the professional football lottery held each year. It will be remembered that, each year, professional football teams conduct a draft of college football prospects. After weeks of scouting (and even the use of computers), the football moguls pick their preferences and send their representatives to the campus for a series of negotiations with the players, which may bring a $250,000 bonus or more to stars like O. J. Simpson or Joe Namath. A good college star can make the team and win a championship.

The corporation draft is less publicized but just as intense. Corporations, faced with a strain on brainpower and manpower for their growth, have looked to the campus for their future leaders and management executives. The importance of this college recruiting program was stated by a General Electric executive who told *Fortune* that "much of our future as a company will depend on our ability to attract the leaders from the campus over the coming years."

The activity is thus well organized. Companies like General Electric, RCA, and Westinghouse send out teams to the schools, prepare literature, brochures, speeches, and billboard displays extolling the virtues of a future career with their company. Student reaction ranges from bewilderment to amusement. The bait is large and the bidding is brisk. Companies offer attractive starting salaries from $7,500 a year and up. Fringe benefits range from free graduate education to insurance policies, vacations, and automatic raises. Interested students get free trips to company headquarters. Defense-oriented companies, with government contracts to push, offer draft-deferred status. A good Negro student will find himself swamped with offers, although few have the real qualifications the job requires.

Yet even among highly motivated students who have toiled

hard for their degrees, life in a big corporation—as a Purdue senior put it, "putting my head in the cog"—is not an easy decision.

Even recruiters themselves have told College Poll interviewers, "The attitude of students has changed. We find them less interested in salary. They want a job that makes them happy. They also want work that is important to them." The recruiter shook his head in surprise. He should not have. Students have been saying this for years, and industry has not been listening.

"I have nothing against bigness in business. Bigness has made America great," said an MIT graduate student. "But bigness carries its responsibilities for service. I want to go with a company that makes a contribution."

Much of the antagonism on the campus is due to the failure of business itself to set its own image straight with the college generation. If students feel that corporations are heartless, it is because of experiences they have had with corporations, or the lack of a proper presentation. It starts with the presentation itself.

"This corporation recruiter spent a whole hour telling me how big his company was, how much it made, how many plants it had, how much the return on capital was, and so forth," said a St. Louis senior. "He never once asked me what I was looking for."

"The offer was conditioned on my willingness to take another course in training," said a Tufts senior. "It's like going to school all over again. All they wanted to do was test me. It would be like taking the College Boards for business."

Not all students reflect negative attitudes. Many find good, well-paying jobs with a big and happy future. These agree with the Yale senior who said, "The trick is to join a smaller company with a growth potential." Or, as a Dartmouth student put it, "There's a lot of money to be made with opportunities that haven't even been discovered yet."

A Miami senior was impressed with the promise, "The re-cruiter explained that his company is making most of its profits from products that didn't exist ten years ago—that's opportunity plus."

Yet even corporate recruiters admit that students want to know what corporations are doing to help solve the social and economic ills of the day. Much of collegiate apathy toward business is directed at industry's preoccupation with profits at the expense of society, and the lack of insight into the students' desire to be of service in their lifetime to help solve them.

Students ask corporate executives directly about their attitudes toward racial discrimination, slum clearance, and social involvement. The college generation is not at all aware of the great strides being made by industry in its efforts to help alleviate the social and economic problems plaguing the public. A special study on corporate images conducted by the College Poll revealed that less then 2 percent of the students could name a specific activity by a specific company in any of the following fields: urban renewal, crime prevention, water and air pollution, racial discrimination, slum clearance, hard-core poverty programs and work pro-grams, etc. Recent campus literature from the corporations is slanted toward contributions in these areas, but the level of penetration is not deep.

Paradoxically, in the same study few students could iden-tify Dow Chemical, or its much publicized product, napalm. A favorite target of the antiwar rioters, Dow Chemical is a virtual nonentity with most students. In fact, many of the nation's multibillion dollar industrial complexes, such as Ling-Temco-Vought, Gulf and Western, and Teledyne are campus unknowns.

This preoccupation with service, for which no generation need apologize, takes on other aspects as collegians face the future. They realize that money is available for work. Ac-cused of being the product of an affluent society, they are

often said to be financially unresponsible—and a kept generation. For those who fear students expect something for nothing, the College Poll study on the guaranteed annual wage
proposal is indicative of basic undergraduate attitudes toward job responsibility.

When asked the question, "Do you believe there should
be a guaranteed annual wage for all Americans?", nearly
seven out of ten students voted no.

"It's a case of something for nothing," said a Case Western
Reserve junior.

"A guaranteed annual wage takes the initiative out of
man," said a Franklin and Marshall economics major. "We'd
be going too far. People have to help themselves."

Students who themselves show a deep concern for the
need for service and happiness in their lives are still deeply
concerned about welfare and its role in society. One might
expect students to favor "handouts" with little controls
for welfare recipients. Quite the opposite. Students feel that
there is need "to get people off relief," and "we must restore
the dignity of the person and the integrity of the people" in
the whole relief program.

Students prefer a job for all rather than a guaranteed
annual wage. "We don't need more handouts. There are
enough relief programs," said a Stanford history major. "We
should get everybody a job. Let them earn their way like
every other American."

College students spend much time and thought on poverty
and the underprivileged. Although campus militants exco-
riate the university for its callous treatment of the poor in
the environs of the campus, students ponder more on how
to actually meet the crises of the cities and the ghettos.
Students work on social programs in their free time, College
Poll studies show. Schools like Bennington, Trinity, Vassar,
and Santa Clara have extensive programs for welfare study.
Students at Buffalo University have established committees

to place minority groups in state construction jobs, like a new campus building. In big urban universities like Chicago and Columbia, social-study programs bring the hard-core poverty programs face to face with student groups. Out of all this stems a growing conviction on the campus that relief alone won't work.

"If we want people to be good citizens, the first requirement is that they believe in themselves. No man or woman can believe in himself if he is supported by relief, or by wages he doesn't earn," said a University of San Francisco student.

With this social awareness, often played up by school newspapers, and constant reminders from student activist groups, the average college student feels he should make a more direct contribution to society. He sees his education as a process to fulfill his life. If he works, he expects a happier, more satisfying life for himself and his family. If he works for a big corporation, he hopes that he will find in his job a substantial contribution to society other than adding to the growth of profits and size. And he trusts that he will be a part of that process.

Students do not have any fear of financial insecurity. They have no basic concern about earning a living or making ends meet. They will tell you that they didn't seek the seeming affluence of their lives. But they feel they are not as dependent on their parents as many would believe.

In inquiring about their contributions, 50 percent admit that their parents pay all of their board and tuition. Of those who contribute to the cost, 22 percent have a scholarship or aid of some sort from school, state, or federal sources. Thirty-seven percent say they have a part-time job either at school or elsewhere. But 85 percent work during the summer or vacation periods, according to the College Poll interviews. Money has been not difficult to earn, and part-time jobs are reasonably plentiful.

It is in this atmosphere that students don't worry about recessions or depressions, a subject of family talk with most students.

Students feel that we will never again have a great depression like we experienced in the 1930s, although they do expect we are likely to have serious recessions that will affect our economy.

The following question was asked of students: "Your parents constantly talk about the Great Depression. Do you yourself think America will ever experience a depression like that again?" Sixty-four percent of the students said no, 34 percent said yes, and 3 percent had no opinion.

"No, I don't think we will ever have another depression like our parents experienced. Our country has too many built-in protections these days," observed a Lowell Tech junior.

"We're not depression-proof. We will always have recessions—and will probably have one soon," a UCLA sophomore commented. "They come in cycles to level off the economy."

Students have only a vague idea of the Great Depression that swept our country from 1929 to 1935. Their impressions of the bleak years come from the conversations they have with their parents and grandparents. But many know of the historical facts behind the economic blight, largely remembered from high school and college history classes.

Asked what they believed caused the Great Depression, most students listed "Wall Street speculation" as the number-one reason.

"People bought stocks that had no real value, hoping to make a killing" was the opinion of a Boston U. sophomore, who is an economics major.

"It was a wild era of speculation and Wall Street caused it, by allowing people to buy stocks with little money" was the opinion of a Ladycliff sophomore.

Other students thought the Depression was the result of "inflation," which caused the panic.

"Prices got too high, people wouldn't or couldn't pay them, and the bubble burst," said a Louisville senior.

Some felt that a "do-nothing government" helped cause the Depression.

"When inflation got too high and the country overproduced, the government had no power to act—and the country drifted into the Depression," declared an Oregon State student.

Few students, however, blame former President Herbert Hoover for the Depression. In fact, few could remember the name of the president who was in office when the stock market crashed.

On the whole, college students see little application to the situation today—and thus only a remote chance of a big depression.

"There are too many built-in stop factors. First there are the controls on the stock market. Then you have the government's controls on prices. And finally, the country is on a better financial basis," explained a Miami U. sophomore.

"The danger would come if the Vietnam War stopped short," a Wisconsin sociology student felt. "With all that war production coming to a halt, business would be cut off and a depression could start. That's one of the reasons we'll have a phase-out of the war and not a quick peace." Many students had a similar view of a tie-in between the Vietnam War and our economic stability.

Students expect that recessions will occur, however, and would not be surprised if one took place in the near future.

"Recessions happen from time to time—and they act as safety valves," said a Houston student.

"It's good to have recessions. They keep things from going too fast," observed a Chicago sophomore. "But recessions hurt the workingman most because industry always uses them as an excuse for cutting wages."

"Recessions are part of the business cycle—a balancing of

supply and demand," said a Princeton junior. "They are like a business fever, a warning that something is wrong."

Asked whether there was too much speculation in the stock market, students had mixed reactions.

"Everybody seems to be buying and selling stocks," admitted a Yale senior. "We even do some brokerage here on the campus. But it makes the market broader and there's less chance of any monopoly selling."

"The lid's going to blow one of these days," was the opinion of a Penn State junior. "Somebody's going to get hurt. These prices are crazy."

Interest in Wall Street, stocks, and business in general is not high on the campus, despite the fact that Ivy League colleges and the larger universities have investment clubs and investment newsletters are distributed on several campuses. Also students with business-oriented courses read the *Wall Street Journal* and business news avidly. The latter newspaper, in fact, operates a college program that is quite active on many campuses, with many students having the paper delivered daily to their dormitories.

On the whole, however, the campus is socially, not business, oriented. Depressions and business cycles are considered more for their social than economic impact.

A Villanova freshman observed that he had heard of the Depression for years from his parents but never appreciated its impact in terms of human misery until he saw *Bonnie and Clyde,* the award-winning motion picture.

"To see people actually evicted from their homes in the film meant more to me than all the talk I ever heard about the Depression. It was stark."

Students who consider their future occupations place teaching high on the list. Nearly 25 percent of all students interviewed stated that teaching was their prime interest as a lifetime career. The popularity of this particular profession waned the longer students were in school. By the time they were seniors only 18 percent placed teaching first.

Students' major interests are, as a matter of fact, immensely varied. Twenty-seven percent chose arts and humanities. Seventeen percent of all students are pursuing social studies. Fourteen percent are studying education. Eleven percent are majoring in some business subject. Less than 5 percent of students are headed for professional studies of any kind, and 10 percent are studying science as a major.

One of the phenomena of the campus today is the great interest in the Peace Corps, which to most students supplies a vehicle for rendering a service.

In addition, as the Peace Corps celebrates its eighth anniversary, it can count on a strong vote of confidence from today's college students for future backing. More than 60 percent of all college students told the College Poll that they would, in principle, join the Peace Corps.

Furthermore, many of those who said they would not join the Department of State's overseas voluntary service organization, gave reasons that indicated support for the corps but unavailability or unsuitability as reasons for not joining.

The question was asked: "Would you join the Peace Corps?" Sixty per cent said yes, 38 percent said no, with 2 percent not answering or with no opinion.

Men are more likely to become Peace Corps members than coeds, and older students—seniors—are more enthusiastic than lower classmen. Negroes are less interested in a Peace Corps tour. Only 30 percent of Negroes said they would join the corps.

Reasons for joining the corps mostly centered upon the following specifics:

A chance to be of service, particularly to the poor.

A good opportunity to learn about other people.

To study and give a person a chance to find himself.

A feeling that by living with other people, respect for America can be gained.

To help fight Communism overseas.

"I believe the Peace Corps may be the only chance a student would ever have to really understand the world," said a Centenary sophomore.

"Having the overseas nations know Americans on a people-to-people basis is the only real chance for world peace" an Iowa sophomore commented.

Not all students are so sure. Among the 38 percent who would not volunteer, there are those who feel that the Peace Corps is a waste of money and talent.

"It's full of misfits who do more harm than good," stated an NYU sophomore.

"Those who can do, do" was the opinion of a Vanderbilt senior. "Those who can't do anything join the Peace Corps."

Many of the more than fifteen hundred Peace Corps returned volunteers have been recruiting on college campuses, and have made a deep impression on the current college generation—far deeper than the commercial recruiter for industry, the College Poll was told.

"A girl who served in Africa spoke at our college, and she obviously had a wonderful experience. She convinced me they are doing a good job," said an Oregon State senior.

Similar reports came about teams who told of specific projects they conducted and the progress they made.

"The people who return make the hardships actually seem worthwhile" was the opinion of a Loyola senior. "I'm not sure I'd join but it seems like a year well spent."

If college students had a choice of overseas posts, the Philippines would be their first choice, the College Poll reveals.

South America, Africa, and Asia are preferred in that order. However, few students want to go to the Congo, or to India, according to a study conducted among students on eighty-seven campuses.

Visiting diplomats from overseas nations have also been visiting American campuses to explain individual needs among the developing nations. These men have made a noteworthy contribution to Peace Corps aims and importance among college audiences.

Many students, particularly those engaged or going steady, would be happy to join if their other half would go. Frequently, however, one of the two is preparing for graduate school or a specific outside career.

"I'd love to go if my fiance would go, too," said a Wisconsin senior, "but he's going to law school next year and I wouldn't want to be away for a year."

Education majors recognize the importance of teaching overseas but some feel their education would be more useful at home.

"I'd find it interesting, of course," commented a Mississippi grammar school teaching major, "but when I realize how much we need teachers here, it seems wrong to neglect our own cities."

Other students prefer VISTA to joining the Peace Corps. These volunteers (who work for the Volunteers in Service to America) feel that they are doing a more direct service to their country. VISTA, called the "domestic Peace Corps," limits its service to the United States.

Students interested in VISTA prefer to work on neighborhood community problems, first with the elderly and with school dropouts next. Service to Indians is lowest in appeal to VISTA's potential recruits.

However, as a Yale sophomore explained, "We'd go where we're sent. It's to be of service where needed that counts. Besides, it's only for a short time."

"I think we have enough problems with our Indians, whom we've neglected for over a century," said a Santa Fe sophomore. "I'd like to help out there for a year."

All in all, the college student of today displays a sincere interest in being of service. It's the idea of how to serve, not whether to serve, that intrigues most students. Few students feel that service in the Peace Corps would be a pleasant adventure. They understand the hardships involved but, as in so many other ways, they indicate to College Poll interviewers a deep-seated interest in assisting their fellowman. That means more than making money to most of the current college generation.

CHAPTER TEN

The College Student
and the Ballot Box

The future of America's political parties may well be shaped by their ability to influence and attract the students now in college. It is certainly true, at the very least, that the current generation will have a large impact on the 1972 presidential election. In many ways, in fact, President Nixon's political future may be in the hands of the students now on university campuses.

Today's college students are political freethinkers. There are seven million of them, all of whom will be eligible to vote in the 1972 presidential election. As of today, nearly 50 percent of those votes are uncommitted to either party.

Previously, students were asked this question in personal interviews on more than one hundred campuses: "Do you consider yourself a Democrat or a Republican—or neither?" Forty-three percent of all students, men and women, said neither.

How these nearly three million uncommitted college students vote in 1972 may swing a close election one way or the other. Additional millions of students will also have come of voting age by that time, and trend studies indicate their political posture would also be largely uncommitted to either party.

College Poll figures show that no political party at this time can claim the support of more than one college student out of four. Students admitting to being party members averaged about 29 percent Democratic, to 27 percent Republican.

Political parties will find a skeptical audience in trying to secure student backing. Neither of the major parties has a strong image with students.

"Neither party appeals to me" or "There's really no difference between political parties these days" are commonplace comments.

Even among students who feel "attached" or identified with either of the major parties, there is little of the party loyalty of previous generations.

"I feel I'm in favor of Democratic party principles," said a Louisiana State senior. "But I don't feel I would have to vote for everyone down the ticket."

This independent thinking is evidenced from the College Poll figures, taken just before the 1968 election, about students following their parents' political beliefs. When students were asked, "Are you generally of the same political belief as your parents?", over half of all students, 55 percent, definitely repudiated their parents' political stances. The remaining students were undecided.

It is evident that incoming freshmen carry with them the influence of their families' political leanings. But this influence wanes as they become older and more independent of home ties. For example, 65 percent of the freshmen interviewed admitted to the same political beliefs as their parents. The percentage drops, however, to 46 percent for seniors.

"I'm going to make up my own mind. Just because my father votes one way or another is no reason for me to follow," explained a Gettysburg junior.

"My parents have followed their party blindly for years. They always vote for the party candidate. They never debate the moral issues," said a Boston University senior.

Even among those students who say they are of the same political following as their families, many insist that they arrived at their decisions through their own choice rather than family influence.

To most students, the political system itself is the subject of grave question, starting with the selection of candidates. In this respect, Senator Eugene McCarthy is a case in point. Paradoxically, most students were not originally for Senator McCarthy, College Poll figures reveal. But when the 1968 campaign started, student frustration over Vietnam and the draft was at an all-time high. Refusal on the part of the administration to halt the bombing and a reluctance to take overt steps to end the war was the talk of the campus, and the rallying cry of campus militants at the time of the emergence of Senator McCarthy as an affirmative force to get something accomplished caused him to be adopted by the campus political activists.

The result was the well-organized campus-backed drive of the senator in the New Hampshire primary, and the abortive campaign for the nomination. The enthusiasm of the senator for the campus as a forum for his ideas led many to believe he was the clear choice of all students. In actual fact, he was not. Nearly 50 percent of students in a College Poll taken this spring admit they never favored Senator McCarthy. But the campus image projected by the senator accomplished many things that explain much of the campus attitudes toward politics, politicians, and political parties.

Many students have indicated that the attention paid to the campus by the politicians and McCarthy's backers was the first major indication to students as to the extent of their own power and the publicity value of campus-oriented campaigns. The impact of the campus endorsement of Senator McCarthy, and the success of the college-spirited drive in New Hampshire was not lost on political campus activists who saw the press, television, and radio representatives swarming over the campus and events being reported out of context.

"The McCarthy campaign taught us a lot," agreed a Columbia S.D.S. member. "We were big news. College was in."

When the drive failed, and McCarthy was dropped by his party, students lost interest in the campaign. The tragic death of Senator Robert Kennedy took out of the political scene the only other candidate of interest in the election. The result was that most students sat out the 1968 political campaign. Nixon, Humphrey, or Wallace created no interest among them. When asked by the College Poll whether they participated in any way in the 1968 elections, 85 percent of all students said no.

With McCarthy out, most students would have voted for Nixon in the campaign if they had the right to vote. The 1968 Presidential Ballot conducted by the College Poll showed that Nixon had the campus vote by 40 percent to 26 percent for Humphrey. Wallace ran a poor third with only 7 percent of the collegiate vote.

Yet there was little enthusiasm for any of the candidates. The majority felt Humphrey was better on liberal issues, but students looked to Nixon "to end the Vietnam War." Students were convinced he would "have a free hand"; "he's a new face in Vietnam"; "he's not bound by the Johnson administration's convictions"; "he's a change."

Some also pointed out that, with Eisenhower, Nixon helped solve the Korean War. To most students, therefore, Nixon will be judged largely on his ability to end the war. Students were also interested in his pledge to bring draft reform and a volunteer army.

But it's the man, not the party, that is the target of their real interest. Incidentally, students voted Senator Muskie as the most promising personality in the 1968 campaign.

When asked, in view of the fact that so many vice-presidents had become president, which man they would prefer as president, Muskie or Governor Agnew, students preferred Muskie by three to one, although they preferred Nixon, Agnew's running mate, as president. Party lines carry no weight or significance for university men and women.

Had Senator McCarthy or Senator Kennedy been running for office, there is little doubt that college students would have had more interest in the 1968 campaign, College Poll interviews clearly indicate.

The other lesson learned by students in the 1968 campaign was their inability to effect direct or quick changes in the political system. With their hard-fought, although brief, campaign for Senator McCarthy going for naught, many undergraduates saw their doubts about the political system itself burgeon alarmingly. Analysts who scoff at students as political amateurs should realize that the 1968 campaign was a test to a considerable number of college men and women—a test that helped confirm their opinion of the Establishment as being responsive to public attitudes.

Public opinion pools revealed that Senator McCarthy could have defeated Nixon at one stage of the campaign. This was after President Johnson had stepped down. All the polls at that time showed that Vice-President Humphrey was a lost shot. McCarthy appeared to have caught the temper of the times, and the press was indicating that the senator, even more than Senator Kennedy, represented the wishes of the Democratic party and the independents. While his poll strength diminished later, it was not until late in the preconvention campaign that students realized the party pros never wanted McCarthy, anyway. He had fought the professionals and that's an unpardonable sin in politics.

Rightly or wrongly, students felt that the political party system selected candidates more by boss direction than by sensitivity to the people's wishes. Students believed that the public, not only students, wanted a McCarthy, or a Kennedy, until he died. The endless television coverage of the conventions, with evasive interviews, secret caucuses, and private deals, produced candidates by "deal," not public demand. Students of all political shades report this reaction.

The tragedy of Chicago to most students was not the riots outside the Democratic Convention hall. Students were much more aware, the College Poll shows, that the riots by the students in the Chicago streets had little to do with the real political issues. Paradoxically, most students (67 percent) have backed the handling of the riots by Mayor Daley and the Chicago police. Students recognized in Chicago the same tactics by a publicity-seeking activist group to gather sympathy for radical causes that had no relevancy to the convention—except to upset it.

Activists on the campus used the Chicago riots to fan antagonism. However, students felt that police who used "excessive" power should be punished. Many declared the police did, in fact, use excessive force and too often reacted to "hate-hippie" impulses. On balance, student opinion clearly condemned violence on either side.

But what most students really found objectionable in the Chicago convention was that "their candidate," McCarthy, never had a chance, despite—or so it seemed to them—stirring victories in the primaries. Also, with Senator Kennedy dead, the only other candidate with the campus appeal was gone from the scene. The result, to most students, was the dreary selection by lackluster politicians.

Following a similar performance in Miami by the Republicans, student enthusiasm for the "system" waned, and is now seriously questioned, though not rejected. Change, in any event, is the order of the day, and students feel change is needed in candidate selection.

Accordingly, they have backed the direct primary to help give the public a more direct choice in the selection of candidates. When asked, "How would you change the selection of candidates for national office?", students voted eight to one for a direct national primary.

Students also feel strongly about their right to vote and

their inability to exercise their franchise, even though they have most of the responsibilities of citizenship. This inability to participate in the ballot box is regarded by them as another denial of their "adult status" inconsistent with the realities of life.

Students have listened with interest and a great deal of skepticism to a parade of politicians of all parties backing the voting program for eighteen-year-olds. They are more aware than their elders realize of the intricate system necessary to bring about actual voting legislation for eighteen-year-olds. Yet it is this very promise and agreement by all as to the fairness of the program, while the necessary implementation is repeatedly blocked, that causes students to question the validity of the system itself.

It is also for these reasons that students become skeptical of politicians and political promises. Students are receptive to honesty and directness in candidates. "Tell it as it is" will be a mandate for any political candidate in the future. Long-winded politicians, speaking in platitudes, not only bore but irk students.

Looking to the future, Senator Edward Kennedy and Mayor John Lindsay appear to be the top candidates with the students. It is their conviction that the 1972 presidential election will be fought between Kennedy and Nixon. However, they believe that the Republican party itself would reject Nixon in the event the Vietnam War were not over.

The trend in politics on the campus is toward liberal rather than conservative thought. Thus to students, the liberal Democratic opinion is represented by Senator Edward Kennedy and Senator Edmund Muskie. Hubert Humphrey, long a liberal, has no real empathy with the college generation. Students have praised Senator Kennedy's stand on most public issues. They were especially impressed with Senator Kennedy's stand on the military decision in Vietnam, wherein he questioned the now historical attack on Hamburger Hill.

Students have no sympathy with the conservative Democratic or Republican politicians. Barry Goldwater, once a campus hero during the President Johnson era, is a virtual campus unknown. Senator Everett Dirksen is popular but recognized as a presidential impossibility, leaving John Lindsay the real champion of Republican undergraduates. Governor Ronald Reagan is liked by most students, but few regard him as a real presidential hopeful. He has also hurt his campus image by recommending force against activists in the California riots. Students may favor arrests for lawlessness, but they abhor the use of tear gas and mace, a policy Governor Reagan has been forced to adopt in California. As a consequence, they feel he has "lost his cool."

There is little enthusiasm for a Third party movement on the campus. The complete failure of the Wallace bid for election is an indication of the basic liberalism of the campus vote. Collegians were familiar with Wallace's basic aims and his aggressive attitudes, which were completely foreign to the mainstream of student thought. The fact that almost half the students could identify the name of his party (the American Independence party) shows their knowledge of the Wallace ploy. Only about 15 percent of the average Americans could identify the party by name, national political polls showed.

The challenge of political parties and politics to the youth in college is to convince them that change within the system can be effected. And equally important, if change cannot be effected, then the system itself can and must be transformed. There is no revolutionary attitude in politics on the campus. Students do not wish to tear down our political systems. There are no more student political activists than there are campus revolutionaries.

A recent statement by George Kennan, historian and former ambassador to Russia, on the subject of change within the system provided a good test of students' attitudes in this area. Students were asked:

"A recent historian has said: 'If you accept a democratic system, it means accepting those things with which you disagree, as well as those things with which you agree. For, if you want to create change in a democratic society, it must be made within the system, or else you'd destroy the system itself.' Do you agree with this statement?" Seventy-seven percent of all students answered yes.

"Of course, or else we'd have chaos," answered a Yale junior.

Even those who answered no had some variation on the answer.

"I'd say no, unless you add that there are circumstances under which the system itself should be changed if it proves, in time, unresponsive to change," said a Cal Tech junior—an opinion which many shared.

In general, however, college students want change, but orderly change.

The danger in politics is not that students will riot at elections; it's that they may stay away. Old-line politicians who wish to attract campus voters will have to alter their appeals to the young voter. Students who have seen much of politics in action evaluate events and personalities with a frankness and directness that, they feel, is absent in political life today.

"Party loyalty" appeals will be ineffective. Students will look to the man, not so much to the party. They will expect action, not words, and will want him to attack problems, not people.

To such candidates, and party, the campus vote could bring the enthusiasm and articulate support that was evidenced somewhat by the "come from nowhere" campaign the students of 1968 waged for Senator Eugene McCarthy. In fact, 1972 is not that far away.

CHAPTER ELEVEN

Do Professors
Wage War?

Most college students, The College Poll shows, are antiwar. They are not necessarily antimilitary. There is quite a distinction between the concepts, and in many instances it is the cause of confusion and concern on the campus.

Take the case of the ROTC. This much-publicized issue is an example of campus pressure groups using student apathy and distaste for war, to create change far beyond the original intent or even desires of the great majority of the student body.

On any afternoon a familiar sight on any given campus is a squad of men marching in formation along the tree-lined walks, or exercising in close-order drill on the parade grounds or football field. Most students accept the scene as a part of their community existence. A very small minority, however, regard the squad as the epitome of military intrusion on the campus.

Although the marchers do not ordinarily appear in uniform, they are part of the ROTC. Chances are they will be dressed in levis and sweatshirts and wear a military hat as they march along. It is all symbolic of the mixed nature of their mission—to be civilians in college, but educated and trained to be reserve officers in one of the branches of service upon graduation.

The program is called the Reserve Officers' Training Corps and was started by the Defense Department several wars ago. It is mostly a volunteer program. Of the 350 colleges and universities now participating in the program, approximately one hundred still pursue some form of compulsory military training—a holdover from the now discarded Morrill Act of 1862 that required land-grant colleges to demand military training of its students. But by and large it is now a volunteer program. In fact, students compete to join—and only about one in ten makes it. This is because of the high physical standards required of all future officers and the drain on students' free time. The program requires several hours a week in military training and attendance at courses in military science.

There are many benefits other than the commission secured upon graduation. The various services award twenty thousand full scholarships through the program. These cover tuition, books, fees, uniforms, plus fifty dollars a month. The thousands not on full scholarships still receive fifty-dollars-a-month pay during the last two years of the program. Many students would not be able to attend college without the ROTC program.

But important as the ROTC is to the student, it is absolutely essential to the services as a source of officer material. In 1968, for example, the ROTC provided more than half of the army's new officer material. Both the navy and the air force secure about 25 percent of their new officers from the campus training program.

The colleges themselves receive little direct benefit from the program except for the student aid provision, and, of course, the service provides all costs including the pay of officers who conduct the course. However, traditionally, campus officials welcome the program as a student and country service. ROTC participants are generally good students and the existence of the ROTC program on a campus is used by many college recruiters as a "plus" in talking to high school graduates.

Regardless of the benefits listed above and the generally favorable administration attitude toward the ROTC, the program may be on the way out. It is under severe attack by the miltant groups on the campus, particularly the S.D.S.

Part of the program's success is due to the fact that most colleges and universities allow academic credit for those military courses taken under ROTC, provided passing grades are achieved. It will be remembered that every student has electives—courses he may take from a rather long list, over and above those actually required for his major subject. In most schools carrying the ROTC program, the Defense Department has requested, and schools have given, academic credit for the military courses as "electives."

The ROTC is actually a contract between the school and the Defense Department. The agreements come up for review regularly. By the time this book appears in print, Yale and Harvard will most likely have notified the Defense Department that any contract renewal will not include the awarding of academic credit for ROTC military-oriented studies. Following this announcement in the spring, John Hopkins, Brown, Princeton, and other schools followed suit.

Most students favor the ROTC and urge the giving of academic credit for the courses, the College Poll reveals.

When asked the question, "Do you think the ROTC belongs on the campus?", 63 percent of all students said yes. Those who objected did so because they felt it was, in some cases, "involuntary and compulsory." On a noncompulsory basis those in favor of the ROTC program increased to almost 80 percent. When asked the question, "Do you think ROTC courses should be given academic credit?", 59 percent of all students answered yes. These questions were asked of students on campuses where ROTC programs were maintained, as well as institutions that do not participate. The difference in percentage between answers was negligible.

"If a guy wants to take on all that work, it's all right with me," was a typical quote.

A Brown senior said, "I can't see it for myself, but it's great for a student who wants to be an officer."

"Why not credit for military subjects? It's as good as Afro-American studies," stated a Houston sophomore.

The S.D.S. campaign against the ROTC reached high gear last fall and in the spring of 1969. Asserting that the "military must go," they campaigned in mass rallies, declaring that the ROTC was a "military foothold" on the campus—another instance of "war-making" on the college scene and the misuse of the university as a cradle of war-makers. They picketed ROTC campus headquarters and, in some instances, jeered ROTC students in formation. But the real issue centered on banning the academic credit for ROTC courses. Realizing that this in itself would eventually cause the program to wither, they made this point a key issue in all student-faculty meetings. Campus and defense officials both admit that the dropping of credit may cripple the program. Students who have to take both ROTC courses and electives will, in the opinion of those concerned, find the program too difficult.

College officials anxious to prevent new confrontations, have turned the issue over to student-faculty advisory boards. These groups, for the most part, have recommended the academic curtailment. College administrations, happy to avoid a possible area of new campus violence, have gone along.

The military is helpless in this area. Any attempt to rally student opinion behind it would be characterized as war-mongering. In fact, the very appearance of military officials on the campus can be cause for reaction. Army, marine, and navy recruiters have all been subjected to picketing and abuse on campuses.

"The military has no place on the campus" was the slogan of the militant students.

The ROTC officer sees it quite differently. Said an army

colonel who teaches in the program, "There are two factors in making an officer today. One is military training. These are the elements most visible to students—the drill, marches, and camp. But this is only one part. The real need is for military education, not training. That's the basic reason to be on the campus. We cannot possibly turn out all our required officers from the service academies. Moreover, we want a balanced percentage of career and reserve officers in our services. This prevents an overload during peacetimes and a supply of educated, trained leaders in reserve for all emergencies. The fact is that we are a civilian army and the ROTC helps keep it that way. The fact is also that we need the ROTC to keep educating officers. That's why these students should continue to get academic credit for military-oriented courses. It's part of their education."

A naval officer attached to the program pointed out another key factor: "The campus is exactly where the program belongs; future officers here lose little of the flavor of collegiate life while pursuing their military duties. They graduated as officers, but the whole thrust of their education has been for life as civilians."

ROTC students are themselves dismayed over the turn of events. With the prospect of extra courses being added to an already crowded schedule, the officer candidates may be forced to drop other activities.

"I think it's an outrage. We are not interfering with anyone else's program or credits. The college should stand behind us on this," commented a Yale officer candidate.

"We are being denied our rights because of the objections of a handful of students who are playing games with our lives for publicity," said a Princeton junior. "The college and Department of Defense should stand up to this one."

"These student boards are loaded with liberal activists," commented a Syracuse junior. "They don't represent real student opinion. Most students don't give a damn about things like this, so these radicals get everything passed. It's an outrage."

There is no evidence that the S.D.S. is satisfied to leave the ROTC drive at denying academic credit. Pleased with their success so far, they are now plotting new moves to get rid of the ROTC entirely.

But if the antimilitarists have success in interfering with the officer supply of the country, even more sensational is their drive against governmental war research on the campuses, which may have even more impact on our overall defense establishment.

In the fall of 1967, the S.D.S. Princeton chapter petitioned President Goheen to drop that university's participation in the Institute of Defense Analysis, an organization of universities working for the Defense Department. Dr. Goheen refused, declaring that the government should have access to the latest and best scientific thinking. The rebuffed S.D.S. then made college defense contracts a campus issue. Using the slogan "Professors Wage War," at a time when the Vietnam War was the prime subject of campus concern, the S.D.S. singled out schools that had defense contracts, and conducted an intensive campaign against the school administrations. Moreover, even in those schools that had no defense contracts, the demand to "dump the Defense Department" was included in the demonstrations and confrontations.

Most students told College Poll interviewers that they agreed with the statement of a Notre Dame senior who said, "The university is the intellectual arsenal of democracy. Any attempt to weaken the flow of scientific help to our government from the campus is a death blow to the defense of our country."

On the other hand, a Columbia sophomore member of the S.D.S. said, "The military has taken over the campus. Defense establishment contracts are stifling our universities and perpetuating war. We must break this contract once and for all."

Students were asked specific questions by the College Poll: "Do you object to your university or college participating in general projects to aid the national defense?" Of those answering, 76 percent said no, 23 percent said yes, and 1 percent had no answer or were undecided.

"The government is entitled to the best brains in the nation for our national defense," stated an MIT senior. "Russia subsidizes military research with direct salaries to all scientists. In our country, by making grants to colleges and universities, scientists are available for both teaching and research."

A Vassar sophomore spoke for most coeds when she said, "There's nothing morally wrong with a professor working for the government if he has a talent or training that is useful for our defense."

Despite the overwhelming vote in favor of university participation in national defense projects, most students object to research that might interfere with teaching students.

Meanwhile, the stiff resentment of the minority 23 percent in the student is prevailing. Moreover, the campus controversy—which has caused more than embarrassment in Washington—has also raised considerable doubt among some faculty members who have been made painfully aware of the fact that their research activities have contributed to a campus atmosphere that in some quarter at least, is antigovernment and antidefense.

There is much at stake. Defense contracts provide almost three-fourths of the funds used by colleges and universities for research. Government grants support science departments, professors, and students. College administrators have agreed that the elimination of these projects—many directly connected with the Defense Department—would vastly curtail scientific study on the campus. Defense officers have watched the controversy grow with a great deal of concern. The fact is that the campus plays a key role in theoretical and applied military research.

The on-campus drive was aided by such off-campus articulate antiwar heavyweights as James Ridgeway, who helped
document the extent of defense-oriented research. His articles in the *New Republic* and *Mayday,* a weekly magazine,
are used by extremist student editors and antiwar demon-
strators. *Ramparts* also helped release heretofore classified
material covering the extent of campus cooperation with the
military. An unfortunate byplay of the release of this information was the widening of the campus credibility gap.
Many university officials who had denied "knowledge" of
contracts were forced finally to admit their existence, despite
the fact that the government had an agreement stipulating
that the activities would be secret or classified.

The antigovernment research campaign has been reasonably successful as far as the militants are concerned. Many
colleges have terminated their programs. Others have agreed
to review their policies. Harvard opted to decline classified
work. The University of Pennsylvania repeatedly reduced
its governmental commitments because of student protests.
How effectual the drive will be in the long run is problem-
atical. Much of the negotiation between colleges and the
Defense Department has to be classified, and research does
go on.

A Midwestern dean explained the collegiate dilemma
eloquently when he said, "The campus is, indeed, the bastion
of theoretical knowledge, much of which is vitally needed
for our defense. Much of the work on the campus is classified
for national security reasons. The work of university laboratories needs no apology for the contribution they have
made, or excuses to any student group. Many scientists are,
indeed, troubled about their role in contributing to weaponry
that causes widespread death and destruction. But until
all people join in a moratorium, the defense of our own nation
requires the continuous exploration of counterweaponry on
a theoretical basis, which is only possible by using the best

scientific brains of our time. These scientists, dedicated men all, naturally gravitate to the university where the pursuit of knowledge in all its forms properly lies.

"Moreover, there is no doubt that we are conducting research in all areas on the campus—social and economic, as well as military. The proper balance is a major political problem of our time, not solved by banners, protests, or confrontations alone. While the enthusiasm of well-meaning, socially conscious youths is helpful in focusing attention on the alternatives, it is hardly time to abandon the Department of Defense, which is charged with the protection of us all from attack and annihilation. We must always be aware of the fact that there are those who would exploit the doubts of the sincere as a pretext to destroying the building instead of fixing the roof."

Although the militance of the minority groups is the guiding force behind these drives, it is easy to overlook the basic attitude of students toward war and militarism and the unpopularity of institutions connected with it.

College students have shared the public doubts over the Vietnam War. But the individual undergraduate, subject to the draft, forced to fight an unpopular war, disillusioned over the continual Vietnam morass, is more articulate in questioning why. In this atmosphere it is easy for militants to charge the ROTC and the campus war laboratories as being extensions of the military plot. While the majority of students may reject the application of guilt by association in these instances, the militants carry on their game against a backdrop of antimilitarism that beats in the hearts of most students.

At the heart of the matter is a broader question—the role of the university itself. Is the university the haven for learning alone, without commitments to other forces or other elements of society? Should it pull back, as demanded by Professor Jacques Barzun of Columbia, into its primary role as a storehouse of knowledge?

It is being used as a tool to perpetuate the military, entrench the Establishment, and impersonalize society?

Students have mixed emotions on those points. The study of the concept of the university is really beyond the interest of most students who really want better teachers, better courses, and meaningful studies. But when it is charged that government research projects do, in fact, interfere with teacher availability, the use of funds that should be spent for learning, the use of space that might be turned into dormitories, and the preoccupation of the administration with outside programs to the detriment of the basic college community, students become interested and aroused. The anti-militarists have deliberately focused on these areas of institutional functions in their confrontations in order to win support from their more conservative colleagues.

Thus it is probably not without merit that the whole area of campus-military relations must be reviewed from time to time, in line with democratic principles. In this respect, student demands, even though they may represent the attitudes of a minority, serve a purpose. However, one of the unfortunate risks involved is that worthwhile programs may be brushed aside, or the rights of the student body at large will be ignored and denied, merely to reach an accommodation with dissidents.

In the final analysis, the College Poll across-the-nation interviews tend to confirm student convictions that the whole role of the campus as the "intellectual arsenal of democracy," while subject to review, should not be endangered merely to bring temporary peace to the campus.

In short, most students don't believe professors wage war. But the Vietnam War has made the military establishment in some areas a campus casualty.

CHAPTER TWELVE

Students View
the World Scene

Relations with Russia are improving steadily and there is little chance we shall ever go to war with Russia, according to the convictions of a majority of university men and women questioned by College Poll interviewers.

Fear of massive retaliation and practical considerations of the nuclear age are the principal reasons for student feelings of optimism against an all-out Russian-American clash.

On the other hand, many caution against a letdown of our guard lest the Russians start "small wars" that could ignite a bigger one.

"Russia knows that war means nuclear war and that means annihilation," said a Georgetown University foreign service major.

"The Russians want peace—they have their own domestic problems" was the way a Baldwin-Wallace sophomore explained the world atmosphere.

When asked the question, "Do you think we'll ever go to war with Russia?", 69 percent of the students said no, and 31 percent said yes.

College students clearly feel that overall relations with

Russia have improved, to the point that the Cold War may be a thing of the past.

"The Soviet leaders are realists. They know they have to get along with the United States," a Penn State sophomore explained.

"The Russians have a new breed of leaders—changed from the Stalin days—and they know the fact of atomic war," said a Villanova freshman.

"The turning point was the Bay of Pigs" was the opinion voiced by a Trinity senior. "When Russians backed down then, it proved that we can stand on fear of retaliation as the safety factor in relations with Russia."

On the other hand, other students are not too sure.

"The Russians are always dangerous and crafty. They could start small wars, in places like the Middle East, and force a larger conflict. They'll gamble on war as a matter of policy, and that could ignite the fuse any place" was the opinion of a Santa Fe sophomore.

A Vietnam veteran who attends Norwalk had an even stronger view on the subject. "There will always be a division in the world over Communism. The Russians are still Communists and that means use of any means to win."

Students are aware of Russia's concern with Red China and the presence of a threat from the East to Russia's border.

"The Russians have a two-thousand-mile Chinese border and they are always worried about the Chinese enemy," said a Dartmouth sophomore. "This helps keep peace in the world and the Russians know it."

College coeds appear less concerned about Russia than college men. On the other hand, college women generally are more conservative than their male colleagues.

Students generally feel that great progress has been made in Russian relations and that it will continue. The current generation, very young in the days of the frigid Cold War, seems quite well versed in Russian politics and policies. Students can name Russia's leaders as well as those of France and England. And modern European history courses, a popular subject on most campuses, cover contemporary Russian history in great detail. Russian is now taught on scores of campuses as an elective language.

The Glassboro conference was cited by many as a good step forward in Russian-American diplomatic relations. Students also are convinced that the Russian participation in the UN helps bridge gaps that might lead to war.

Danger points of Russian-American relations are, in the students' opinion, the Middle East, Germany, and Vietnam.

"The Middle East is a testing ground. If we can solve the problems there, we could have peace for many years," stated a Washington State senior.

"The Russians are arming the Egyptians and we're arming the Israelis. That's bound to blow up soon and, if it does, it could spread this time," said a Columbia sophomore.

An Ohio Wesleyan sophomore is worried about Germany. "That's the starting point of so many wars. The Russians fear the Germans and until the Berlin problem is solved and the German treaty signed, it could cause war."

Stalin is pictured on the campus as a bleak, barbaric man who reigned in the tradition of a feudal czar. A great number of students are familiar with the Stalin purges and cite them as representative of the old Russian government.

Intercultural exchanges are cited by many students as a means of prompting understanding between the countries. Students at larger universities, who often see ballet and choral groups from overseas, are usually enthusiastic about exchange programs.

The Bolshoi Ballet, in particular, is mentioned frequently by students as an example of an ideal exchange program. They also think our current folk singers would be well received and understood by Russians.

Students do not consider Russians inferior to Americans,

although they recognize that the Russian people have a lower standard of living. The current college generation, however, does not place much value on material things. As for the success of the Sputnik program, it is referred to by students as proof of Russia's military and engineering capability.

There is great interest in the Russian populace—as evidence by campus opinion in favor of establishing a broader dialogue with the Soviets—a people-to-people basis—but Russian politics are looked upon with a wary skepticism.

While college students feel that Russian relations with the United States and the world are improving, they still express concern about dropping behind the Iron Curtain personally, the College Poll shows.

When asked, "Would you have any doubts about visiting Russia as far as your own safety was concerned?", nearly four out of ten said yes, four out of ten said no, and two out of ten were undecided.

On the other hand, six out of ten collegians said they were interested in going to see Russia. But it was far down the list of countries the students preferred to visit. Switzerland, Italy, France, and the Netherlands, Ireland, and Germany were listed ahead of Russia.

But if Russian relations are hopeful, China is a dark cloud in the East. The United States eventually will have to go to war with Red China in the opinion of nearly seven out of ten U.S. college students, the College Poll reveals. The study points out campus fear of Red Chinese "intractability" and her recent development of atomic- and hydrogen-bomb capability as the key danger point of SINO-America relationships that will lead, eventually, to war.

However, students were equally clear that admission of Red China to the United Nations, and establishment of dialogue with the Peking regime, would go a long way toward helping to pierce the Bamboo Curtain.

Failure of Chinese Reds to keep their date in Warsaw last

spring was considered a serious indication of deteriorating relations. This was America's first scheduled diplomatic meeting with Red China in more than a year, and, many diplomats feel, presented a potential breakthrough in Chinese-American relations, especially for the new administration.

While the opinion reflected in the poll is pessimistic, it is not exactly hopeless. But fear of Red China as an irresponsible nation remains widespread on the campus.

"Red China is on a collision course with the whole world. It will be up to us and Russia to stop them," warned a Kansas senior.

"Red China is a have-not nation—and the Chinese will use any force or weapon to get what they want" was the opinion of a Georgia Tech sophomore.

But even if most students fear Red China's strength, they are not sure that Peking is as irresponsible as its reputation would imply.

"Red China doesn't want war," said a Temple sophomore. "She hasn't intervened in Vietnam except to give aid. And, she didn't help North Korea until her borders were threatened."

"The Peking Government is too involved with internal problems. What we have to do is not provoke another Korea or Vietnam and bring peace to the Asians. That will give us time to negotiate with Red China like we have with Russia in the UN" was the opinion of a New York University political science major.

The advent of Red China atomic capability concerns many students who feel an irresponsible Red China may force showdown situations.

"They'll never agree to any test-ban treaty or any limit of their use of the bomb," a Michigan State sophomore declared. "The only thing the Chinese will respect is strength. And when they are ready, we will have to be prepared for a series of showdowns like we had in Cuba with Russia."

The importance of maintaining a close relationship with Russia in controlling China was also stressed.

"The Russians fear the Chinese Reds more than we do. They have four thousand miles of border with the Reds, and need a million troops to protect that border," said a Villanova freshman. "The more Red China is a threat, the better the chance for world peace. Russia would never want to face a two-front war the way Germany did."

Students also are well aware of Red China's attempts to sell the Red Chinese brand of communism to the world.

"The Peking government is working deals in Cuba and in Africa," explained a Tufts history major. "They have agents everywhere—even more than the Russians. You'll see the Red Chinese banners in the parades at every uprising throughout the world. They are dangerous people."

Other students point out Red China's lack of value for human life. They indicate that the millions of people who are massacred behind the Bamboo Curtain are reason to fear the Red Chinese people as irresponsible and a danger to world peace.

But, if the students are wary of Peking and the good faith of the Red Chinese, they place much hope in the UN as a key to arriving at a détente with China. They disagree with President Nixon's campaign speeches, which called for rejection of a Chinese bid to the UN but left the door partly open. Students would go further than mere admission and give the Peking government of Red China full recognition.

"They are, in fact, the government of the Chinese people," stated Houston sophomore. "Denying recognition is merely a way of keeping us apart and constitutes a danger through misunderstanding of objectives. Besides, the British have been trading with Red China for years."

"Keeping Red China out of the UN because of Chiang Kai-shek is a foolish policy," according to a Miami senior. "Taiwan is in existence only because we support it. Chiang is an old man—and there is no chance he'll ever reconquer China."

Students see no problem in keeping Taiwan in the UN as a Republic of China nation. "It should be admitted as Formosa—just like Canada and Australia have separate memberships, although they are in the U.K.," a Washington State economics major advised.

The hope for a new regime arising out of the recent civil war in China was expressed by some students. "Mao Tsetung is a man of the past. Perhaps Red China will reject his doctrines like the Russians rejected Stalinism after he died," a Boston College freshman suggested.

American college students see no parallel between the confrontations on the American campus and the youth uprisings in Red China. The Red guards are branded as revolutionaries by most American students, who term the American college riots as collegiate reform with no political overtones. In fact, previous College Poll reports show that most American college students reject violence as a way of achieving student objectives.

Students appear to be well informed about Red China. The majority of the queried could give the exact name of the Peking government (People's Republic of China) and knew a great deal about Mao and recent Chinese history. Many students referred to a "natural aversion" of Chinese to the Western world that will make negotiations in the coming years difficult.

By like token, there seems to be little affinity for the Chinese, of any political denomination, among American college students. Few are anxious to visit China, or even appear interested in Chinese as an academic discipline. Although there is fear of possible war with Red China, there is no prejudice against the Chinese as a people.

When asked whether the Chinese minority was discriminated against on the campus, nine out of ten students said no. In fact, students feel that there is not much campus bias at all. They do not relate American-Chinese with their Peking relatives, and have little or no identification of Chinese as other than "Americans." However, all agree on the need for a broader dialogue with Chinese on all levels.

In summary, Red China is regarded as a real threat to peace. Red Chinese officials are a sinister, remote, and ruthless group, who would be reckless in the application of atomic power. Only through the UN, and recognition of Red China as a fact of life in world affairs, can the Red Chinese be brought into the world community, and a dialogue created that would lead to understanding and peace.

The UN itself, however, is a source of concern to the college generation who admires its concept and structure but denigrates the organization for the way it is performing its function.

"How can you say the United Nations is doing a good job when there has been a war going on in Vietnam for five years and the UN is powerless to stop it?" asked an NYU junior with a display of indignation.

"It's not possible to have a UN without having all nations, including Red China, as members," a Kansas State senior added.

These two views coincide with those expressed by a majority of U.S. college students questioned by the College Poll.

When asked the question, "Do you think the UN is doing a good job?", students voted 68 percent no, 30 percent yes, and 2 percent undecided.

But it should not be inferred that students would outlaw or change the world organization in principle. The prevalent attitude is to strengthen the assembly itself. Moreover, college students showed a broad knowledge of the United Nations program.

Failure to stop the Vietnam War was the most frequently

quoted reason given by the students for the lack of confidence in the world organization. "They don't even have a delegate at the Paris talks," bemoaned a Northwestern coed.

"The UN has some great programs for health and underdeveloped nations, but its basic role is to keep the peace and in this endeavor it has failed," said a Boston University senior.

"The Taiwan government is a fiction. Red China is a fact of life. The UN is being handled like a club. Admit those whom you want," said a Georgetown University foreign service major.

On the other hand, many students support the role of the UN and particularly the efforts of the secretary-general. Many feel we have ignored the UN in its attempt to bring peace in Southeast Asia.

The prompt settlement of the Middle Eastern war was credited to the UN. And there was almost a unanimity of opinion to the effect that the world organization helped prevent many disputes from breaking into open warfare.

On the other hand, there was frequent criticism of the United States' own role in the organization. The general consensus was that, in principle, the United States and Russia use the assembly as a tool for their own interests.

"We go along with the Security Council when we want to," said a Harvard political major. "And so does Russia. But we also go our own way regardless of what the UN thinks— like in Vietnam."

"We really can't give up our sovereignty to the UN, but we could back it more than we do," commented a California coed.

"If the Vietnam War is not settled, the United States is just as responsible as anyone else, not the UN," observed a Syracuse University history major.

An Ohio Wesleyan coed said, "The United States has used

the veto power as much as anyone. The UN has done all it could do in Vietnam."

"Secretary U Thant urged us to stop bombing more than a year ago and said that it would bring peace talks," commented a Detroit U. sophomore. "If we had listened to the UN then, the war might be over now."

Students feel that, for all its weaknesses, the UN is a necessary forum and even those who accuse the UN of doing a poor job do not urge its abolition. The necessity for a world organization of some sort is almost universally accepted on all campuses.

In discussing the role of the United States in the UN, it was generally agreed that the U.S. ambassador representing this country at the world organization should have more authority. Of the recent ambassadors to the UN, Adlai Stevenson seemed to be the most admired, with Ambassador Arthur Goldberg next.

However, further questioning by College Poll reps brought out the belief that the role of ambassador to the UN is not to exert the influence of the United States as a moral and political force in the world, but to act as a spokesman for the State Department.

"Look at Ambassador Stevenson; he had no real authority in the UN," pointed out a Georgetown U. School of Foreign Service student. "And Ambassador Goldberg publicly stated that he had no real power and wanted out. It should be the most prestigious job in the United States next to the president."

"We never really have used the UN for the force it embraces. If we really put our whole power behind our decision in the Security Council, much more would be accomplished," declared a Columbia junior.

Most students expressed a willingness to support a proposal to make the UN delegate an elective office. When asked, "Should the public vote on the U.S. delegate to the United

Nations?", students answered yes 65 percent to 31 percent. The remaining students were not sure.

Those who agreed felt that the "delegate would have more power since he was selected by the people."

Yet others felt it would be "unwise" or 'impractical" or as a Stanford senior said, "It's like electing the Cabinet. It's a president's privilege to select his aides."

The vote, however, showed concern about the personality, politics, and power of our UN representative.

Students also have a deep interest in NATO. The bulk of them believe that NATO has done a good job. When asked to rate NATO's performance, 68 percent said it was good to excellent, 30 percent said poor, and the others had no opinion. Most students could identify NATO. They resented France's blocking of many NATO programs and the attitude of General De Gaulle in particular. In fact, campus opinion about France was generally negative.

"They forgot fast all we did for them," said many students. Other students felt that France's ties with Russia made her a dangerous ally of the United States. Many have read a book called *Topaz*, a novel dealing with a spy leak in NATO affairs. Many referred to it in College Poll interviews.

The CIA, incidentally, is hardly the villain that the S.D.S. would have the public believe. When asked to rate the Central Intelligence Agency, most students backed the organization with a 67 percent favorable vote. Their attitude toward "spying" in general was noncommittal. Many simply regard it as "a necessary fact of life."

The College Poll reveals that students have a broad interest in international affairs. Certainly the Vietnam War and the draft have made them vitally concerned about the course of our international commitments.

"All in all, they are well read and exposed to news and news media more than their parents were, for example," explained a New York college president. "Of course, many travel extensively, and many of their parents and friends do likewise. The world has gotten smaller and the college student today is vitally interested in seeing and learning all he can about it. This attitude is encouraging and represents a real hope for the free world."

CHAPTER THIRTEEN

Hair, Hippies, and Heroes

"I generally get a haircut just before I go home—just to keep peace," confessed a Fordham social studies major. "You know I can get straight A's, make the dean's list, get elected Student Council President—but let me come home with long hair and my parents think I'm a bum. Of course, I'm not making straight A's either," he added.

But it's a true analysis of parent-student relationships that the divergent ideas about hair seem to be a constant source of irritation. To the college generation, at least, it is a symbol of parental preoccupation with externals. It is also an excellent example of the manner in which the older generation concentrates on tradition and total conformity as the basic standard of life—and ignores the personal preferences and wishes of the individual—in the students' view.

Students feel that how a person wears his hair is his own business. It's a style, not a symbol of protest, to most students. They may not agree with their classmate—they may not even like him—but they won't disagree or dislike him merely because his hair is long. Most parents will dislike him immediately only for this reason. Students regard this as hypocrisy and prejudice, and if it applies to an individual, it applies to color, money, religion, and the whole gamut of externals. This view is shared not only by hippies, but by most students—even those who prefer crew cuts themselves. It is an attitude few parents understand. Interviews reveal that underneath most collegians admit they make an issue of it because theirs is so just a position that it helps dramatize parental intransigence.

"Thomas Jefferson wore long hair and he became president of the United States," said a Berkeley junior to the College Poll interviewers.

"Many of our really great creative people wore long hair. Look at Carl Sandburg and Albert Einstein. They weren't hippies," said a North Carolina economics major.

"I don't think it is long hair that makes a man a hippie," observed a Boston University coed. "It's when he doesn't wash that irks me."

These views are typical of collegians, as the ratio of affirmative replies to the following query will affirm:

"Do you believe that long hair is proper for a male university or college student?"

Of those answering, 64 percent said yes, 33 percent said no, with 3 percent not answering or not sure.

"People are making too big a thing about student hair styles," commented a Vanderbilt sophomore. "We take people as they are. If a guy wants to wear his hair long, that's his business."

"The complaints that people have about long hair is typical of the shallow minds of the older generation," complained a Harvard sophomore. "They want easy ways to categorize people, so they typecast a whole generation as no good because it wears long hair. It is to laugh!"

Students differ as to the origin of the long hair and beard fad on the campus. Some feel that it is just a matter of style change that occurs every generation or so. Some indicate it is a visual protest against the Establishment.

"It's like short skirts and long skirts," said an NYU marketing major. "Styles and fashions change. Long hair is basically a change of style, not a revolution. It symbolizes the times—the freedom of the age, but only because it is change, not revolt."

Others disagree. "They do it deliberately. Long hair is the symbol of revolution—a *de facto* act of revolt against the conformist philosophy of the day," said a Yale sophomore. "It rejects the ritual of haircutting—a tradition both as tribal and heathen as the cult of purification by bloodletting."

"Wearing hair in the natural state is a healthy return to the basics of human living—free from the cosmetic influences of a decaying society," observed a University of Illinois sophomore, who boasted a full head of uncombed hair himself.

"The Beatles started it" was the opinion of a Missouri University sophomore. "They made the hippie hair a fad and it just picked up momentum."

Many students expressed the view that long hair is really the preference of two types of students, each quite different from the other.

"I guess we have all but rejected the crew cut, which is after all, the G.I.'s uniform," explained a University of Delaware senior. "But long hair doesn't necessarily mean a beard and a head rug. Sideburns and a reasonably long cut is what most students wear. It's comfortable and seems to fit into the styles of the day."

A more practical view was expressed by a Tulane senior. "Frankly, I let my hair grow longer to save money. It costs $2.50 a haircut at the campus barbershop and if I let it grow I trim it myself. If I got the regular haircut, I'd be there every two weeks."

Most students reported that their parents are unhappy about long hair. However, they also note with considerable interest the impact college styles are having on the older generation.

"Last Christmas when I went home, my dad had sideburns!" revealed a Stanford junior. "You can't imagine what a change that is in his thinking. He looked pretty sharp, too."

"Maybe we can get something changed," commented an Oregon State junior. "I went to my father's office over the holidays and saw that many of the men had longer hair. Two years ago my father would have fired them."

Coeds have quite different ideas about men's hair. Most girls seem to accept and prefer the longer cut of the contemporary hair styles, but hippie lengths are out.

"If you're a love girl yourself, the boy's hair doesn't make any difference," said a Goucher senior. "But you feel as if you're with a freak when he has long hair and you're in public—no matter how nice he is. Everybody looks at you."

"College men who wear very long hair are out to prove something," a Georgian Court sophomore insisted. "And they aren't much fun on dates. I guess most girls like boys who are going places, but able to adjust to society more."

"They are dirty" was the blunt, emphatic comment of a pretty University of Buffalo coed.

Students themselves are not unaware of the public attitudes toward hair styles. They know that it may affect their job potential.

"We had a recruiter who came to sell us on going with a big corporation," said a Penn State sophomore. "He told us point-blank that long hair is out. It's like walking in with a guitar under your arm to get a bank job. Well, we know that and eventually I guess we'll have to cut the hair to get bread."

Meanwhile, college officials seem to view the scene with comparative calm.

"It's an inoffensive form of protest," observed a Midwestern dean of men. "We try to worry about more serious forms of protest. But it has hurt the income of the campus barber."

A Harvard professor laughed it off. "You know, in my day we ate live goldfish."

Attitudes toward long hair match those relating to hippies and odd campus-dress styles. Most parents would be shocked if they saw how their sons and daughters dress on a day-by-day basis. While magazines are filled with pictures of well-dressed collegians, wearing the latest styles, few actually live that way. While Ivy Leaguers and some of the more expensive schools boast a number of dudes, most students dress casually on campus.

It's a wash-and-wear generation. Many college males live in blue jeans and desert boots or loafers all through school. School jackets help give a uniformity to campus clothes—a symbol of conformity that is often welcomed. The girls at Vassar or Skidmore are just as likely to wear jeans since these schools are more lenient about classroom and campus dress. Few girls' colleges still require the coeds to wear stockings, although it is questionable whether jeans or miniskirts are more controversial or diversionary. Practically no school requires a tie and jacket for men. Campus life is informal. Affluence is measured more by owning a car than by fancy clothes. But even affluence means little to today's more democratic student body.

Day hops—students who live at home—tend to dress more conservatively. After all, they must face their parents every day. But the young man who leaves home for months at a time exercises his freedom in many ways, almost always in dress and haircut.

"Few hippies live at home" was the statement of a California dean—and it is probably true.

"Not for long, anyway," added a hippie when he heard about the statement.

Actually, most students object to the term "hippie."

"Go ahead, define a hippie" was the frequent start of a dormitory bull session. "Is Bill a hippie?"

When pressed, most students will agree that a hippie is one who dresses extremely as a way of protest. But there is considerable concern because parents and the older generation arbitrarily categorize those who dress differently as radical and society rejects. It's not always true, particularly on campus.

"A hippie is a hippie—and his hairdo and dress are not popular on campus. But we don't condemn him just for that. Many of the hippies are bright guys and full of ideas," said a Santa Fe student.

To the argument that such individuals don't belong in college, students make a quick rebuttal.

"Colleges is just where they do belong. College is for questioning and deciding. They are questioning everything and eventually they decide. If they want the life of a hippie—to live a life of protest—that's their decision. At least they are honest."

Thus, collegians display a sort of respect for the individual who questions, and has the courage or willpower to stand up for it.

"Many of us say we want change, but the hippie is trying in his way to bring it about," stated a Miami student. "I don't agree with him, but he has guts."

"If you realize that the love people are trying an experiment, you'll understand them better," explained a Monmouth junior. "They feel that you can build a world on love for each other. They reject the world's hate as expressed by war, crime, and oppression. Now, I don't believe it's possible either, but you have to respect the fact that they're trying."

Students are quick to defend any person who seems sincerely dedicated to an ideal. In campus discussions about communal farms, for example, College Poll interviewers were told:

"It's free love—not sex—that the hippies practice," observed a Michigan State junior. "Now that's not the kind of life I'd want, nor would I want my family to have either. But if they agree they want to try an ideal life—an experiment—why not? We've studied many such experiments in college, and from between the lines we can see it wasn't so different then.

Oneida was a noble experiment. Today those people would be jailed."

"Just because hippies withdraw from society into a communal life, that doesn't make the process wrong in itself. Monastics withdraw, too. That's not wrong either. They are all trying for something purer and better, even if it means disgrace or banishment from society," commented a St. Joseph sophomore.

However, there are ample collegians who take a completely divergent view as the following statements reveal:

"They need a bath and a haircut and a good clout," grumbled a Stanford junior.

"The hippies are afraid of life. They are giving our generation a bad name," a Harvard senior noted.

"They're no flower people. They are more like weeds in the garden," said a Loyola senior. "Were you ever aware that people noticed weeds before they notice flowers?"

It is interesting to note, however, that almost all students agree that hippies should not be "beyond the law." Furthermore, collegians are generally inclined toward tolerance, particularly in the willingness to give all sides in a debate an opportunity to be heard.

"Let them speak out," is no idle campus dictum. Students practice what they preach. It is rarely reported that the campus lecture platform is open to all shades of public opinion and dogma. During any given week, a cross section of current thought, as personified by such speakers as Senator McCarthy, Senator Dirksen, and Arthur Schlesinger may appear on campus seminars. Abbe Robinson, Stokely Carmichael, and other black leaders are also invited to speak at many universities.

Students not only want to tell it as it is. They want to hear it as it is. These lectures are usually arranged by students themselves and paid for out of student-contributed funds.

"We don't learn anything at the commencement addresses,"

reported a student leader at Penn State. "We want people to talk out—not preach. We want to hear their side and let them listen to ours. It works, too. We're getting terrific reaction from the students who pay their own money to listen and learn."

Speakers who are invited to campus forums are watched carefully by local police and federal authorities. Students take great precautions to ensure safety measures for them, even going so far as to recommend that they come "without a sympathetic group"—to prevent a possible uprising such as the one that recently occurred at an Indiana college. Few incidents have occurred as a result of these lectures. In any event, this open-forum approach has enabled the college community to assimilate the background and thinking behind the "other side" of all issues. And the platform dialogue continues. A heavy lecture schedule was set for the fall, 1969, semester at more than five hundred colleges and universities.

Many people erroneously believe that college students are making heroes of the wrong people. Accordingly, they fear that in defending the rights of hippies, the Black Panthers, and free lovers, collegians may be losing their perspective. The College Poll shows otherwise.

When asked: "What living American men do you admire most?", students selected Senator Eugene McCarthy and Senator Edward Kennedy as the most admired, each drawing approximately 14 percent of all votes. Next in line were John Lindsay, President Nixon, Bob Hope, Senator Everett Dirksen, President Lyndon Johnson, and Hubert Humphrey. Far down on the list were such Establishment names as Averell Harriman, Vice-President Spiro Agnew, and newscasters Chet Huntley and Walter Cronkite. Mayor Richard Daley was eighteenth. Also near the bottom were Stokely Carmichael and the "high priest of the radicals"—Herbert Marcuse. Even Vince Lombardi and Arnold Palmer placed higher.

Comments on their choices were interesting and revealing.
On Senator Eugene McCarthy: "He stood up for what he believed in—even challenging the president."

"He's a symbol indicating you should try to make the system work—even if it didn't."

"He showed courage and understanding."

On Senator Edward Kennedy:
"He's got all the courage of his brother and even greater compassion."

"He's the hope of the generation—and to stay in the fight after what he's been through is an inspiration to everyone."

On President Nixon:
"Although he was licked badly several times, he never gave up."

"He's our president. We have to admire a president who won a fair fight."

On Bob Hope:
"He's never lost contact with the people who are fighting for our country."

"He gave up every holiday to be with the servicemen."

On John Lindsay:
"He's got class. The New York job was impossible, but he fought for principle."

"He's a man of integrity. He never gave in to the bosses."

On President Johnson:
"He tried his best."

"He gave up his job to help solve the war. He'd have been reelected for sure."

"He had trouble following John Kennedy. But he tried."

Students were asked what living American women they admired most.

Most interviewees selected Mrs. Martin Luther King first, with 22 percent of the vote going to her. Next was Mrs. Robert F. Kennedy, with 16 percent, followed by Mrs. Rose Kennedy, with 14 percent. Next was Margaret Mead, polling 13 percent, followed by Mrs. Aristotle Onassis, with 9 percent. Others were Mrs. Richard Nixon, Dr. Joyce Brothers, Mrs. Dwight Eisenhower, Mrs. Lyndon Johnson, and Mrs. Harry Truman.

All in all, the college student wants to accept people as they are, not on the basis of what they wear, how they live, or what color they are. They don't necessarily want to change their own lives to fit the lives of others. But they do want to understand so that they can achieve greater fulfillment in their own lives, and fit better into the world as it is.

CHAPTER FOURTEEN

Are Fraternities
and Sororities
on the Way out?

Every year, the executive secretary of one of the leading national fraternities, established before 1850, makes a tour of chapters at leading colleges and universities. His job is to carry the message of tradition, brotherhood, and dedication to the new members. He also inspects the chapter house, meets chapter officers, gathers information for the fraternity magazine and, in general, helps cement the ties with the national office. He may even help install some new members, observing a secret ritual now generations old. After he completes his visit, he prepares a report for headquarters in New York.

It is often a shocker—enough to shake the ivy from the the walls of the national office. These days a visit to a local chapter can be a harrowing experience for an old grad. All too often the secretary finds the chapter down in numbers, deep in debt, the fraternity chapter house in need of repair, and operating at a loss. What is even more important, he discovers that the venerable fraternity, one of a dozen national fraternal organizations at the college, has hit a low in campus prestige.

The fact is that national fraternities, particularly the Greek letter groups (called the "Greeks" on most campuses) have fallen on hard times.

The old Roaring Twenties fraternity days of the movies, when fraternity brothers sat in secret sessions and selected the cream of the new students for glory, leaving the rest to social oblivion, have passed.

Not that the fraternities, and to a lesser extent sororities, are not still important groups on the campus scene. They have a long tradition, dating back to 1776 when Phi Beta Kappa was launched at William and Mary. Oddly enough, Phi Beta Kappa is still one of the most respected of all fraternities; its familiar Greek letter key is a badge of scholastic honor both on and off campus. There are more than sixty other national fraternities, and a lesser number of sororities, some nearly one hundred years old, that have accumulated tradition, prestige, and even wealth over the decades. These have more than thirty-five hundred chapters across the country, with hundreds of thousands of members.

In addition, there are hundreds of local fraternities, which have appropriated their own Greek letters, but consist of only one chapter. These groups, also many decades old, were started for special aims—professional, social, educational, and even athletic.

Campus-to-campus membership is uneven. Ohio Wesleyan University, for instance, boasts that 90 percent of its male students belong to chapters of the fourteen national and several local fraternities on the campus. It also points out that 85 percent of all coeds are affiliated with the dozen or so sororities with local chapters.

On the other hand, many colleges have no fraternities or or sororities. Some of them—like Princeton, where fraternities are not permitted as such—maintain exclusive eating clubs. Yale has its secret societies and Harvard its exclusive clubs that have polarized student activities into exclusive groups for nearly a century.

In any event, the influence of national fraternities and sororities is waning on the campus, and this reduction of campus power has hurt the "Greeks," and helped the local organizations. In addition, the entire character and function of the traditional fraternities on the campus is changing, according to interviews conducted by the College Poll.

When asked this question, "Are fraternities or sororities of growing or lesser importance on the campus?", 63 percent of all students answered lesser, 28 percent said growing, and 9 percent had no opinion or were not sure.

Many are convinced the change is overdue. For decades past, many a student on the way to college was warned by parents to waste no time in getting pledged into a good fraternity or sorority. It was a good advice. In those days, fraternities and sororities often controlled campuses, socially and politically. Traditionally, fraternities were, in fact, founded to help control campus elections—which were an area of concern back as far as 1835. Although in later years fraternities have taken a somewhat broader view of their contributions to campus life, on the whole, fraternity membership meant making it or breaking it during one's college career. Students who were passed by in pledging often left school. And justifiably or not, many a student carried these rejections as a psychological handicap through life. For fraternities and sororities not only controlled elections and appointments to salient activities, but also provided the all-important key to campus status—living in the fraternity and sorority house.

The chapter house had become both the symbol and center of campus social success. Girls vied to attend fraternity parties. In the years since 1900, fraternity houses became the students' home away from home, isolated from the rest of the campus by secret rituals and a fraternal bond that more often than not survived graduation.

They served their members well. To the new student, the fraternity brothers provided a warm group to help him adjust to campus life, and assist in resisting loneliness. Moreover, they aided in developing social and, at times, academic survival. Alumni concern for graduating brothers often

meant profitable business introductions, adding future promise to membership. Returning alumni at college reunions
heaped advice and largess on local chapters. In some cases
they endowed fraternities, built and leased to chapters many
of the imposing buildings on or near campus. Some maintained employment bureaus, published magazines, and
helped guide graduate careers through active committees.
To the college and university itself, the continued interest
in fraternal life by the alumni has helped build endow-
ments and class-giving.

The fraternity prestige reached its zenith shortly after
World War II. Up to that time, students, both male and female, enjoyed the prestige of pledging and being vied for
selection by the most influential groups.

But change in the fraternity life has come to the campus
scene—and most dramatically in the past few years. The
reasons are many. The principal cause is clearly the inherent
prejudice of national fraternities that considered race, creed,
and color as criteria for membership.

College authorities, who have the right to recognize or
forbid the existence of fraternities, started pressures some
years ago to have civil rights principles adapted to the campus fraternity and sorority pledging system.

The national fraternities, in particular, refused to admit
blacks and other minority groups. When local chapters
acted on their own, they fought back—using their alumni
and national organizational task forces. A Stanford chapter
of Sigma Chi was suspended by the national office for accepting blacks. They also acted against chapters at Brown
and the University of Chicago for similar local indiscretions.

However, they misinterpreted the temper of the students
on the campus. The publicity was played up on all college
campuses, and the result was the lessening of respect for all
Greek-letter national organizations. Many colleges like Wil-
liams actually abolished most of the fraternities. Amherst,

following a critical faculty report, has recommended similar action.

Since then, student apathy toward national "Greeks" has grown on most campuses. This year, Stanford failed to fill its quota. Other California colleges that have felt the impact of "anti-Greek" movements more than most, are faced with empty fraternity houses, many of which are in disrepair and being operated at a loss.

Sororities, too, have felt the change of coeds' attitudes. While their numbers have not been drastically reduced, the sorority-dominated campus is rare indeed.

"We find girls are not too anxious to live in segregated quarters in today's collegiate atmosphere," reported a national sorority secretary. "The growing trend toward co-educational living facilities makes the sorority house less inviting to the new students."

More realistically, today's coed, the College Poll shows, shares the desire of male collegians to live a less status-oriented life. The blackballing of students because of race or religion is rejected merely because it creates an "unreal life" on the campus and in the group. It was this blackballing system, based upon standards set up by national groups, that irked most students.

Until recently, in large universities like Minnesota and Wisconsin, for example, there was not a single Negro in any fraternity, although student bodies collectively totaled more than one hundred thousand students. A black fraternity has been started at Minnesota, and changes have since been made in other schools.

The democracy of the college campus has changed the function of the fraternity. With emphasis on social superiority disappearing, and the stranglehold on student governments broken, the student looks to a fraternity and sorority as it really is—a group or clique created for a particular purpose. Students place these societies in proper perspective and do not expect too much of them except "involvement with a compatible group."

"The 'Greeks' are a lot of phonies," a Northwestern sophomore put it. "Our local fraternity is a well-rounded group and we have a great time."

This attitude, which reflects the more mature and individualistic role of the fraternity or sorority, has made the local fraternity more acceptable, and forced the national "Greeks" to lower their bars. As far as the average student is concerned, the old-line fraternity is another form of Establishment—a rigidly conforming institution that sets a tone for future life most students hope to avoid.

Also to be considered is the fact that today's college students represent a broader base of American society than the college men and women of several decades ago, when the closed fraternity system flourished. Only a small percentage of Americans went to college in those days, and they represented a higher income and a more socially conscious group than today's more democratic student body.

Local fraternities also resent controls by national groups in areas other than those concerning membership requirements. Returning alumni fraternity members find they have little in common with today's free-swinging brothers and sisters.

"The generation gap becomes pretty well defined when we try to tell some of these chapter heads what to do," admitted a national secretary. "We're out of tune with today's campus life—and we'll have to adjust to survive."

Many are trying, and succeeding quite well. Harvard's exclusive clubs have changed admission requirements.

"They have not been lowered," emphasized a club president. "They have become more realistic and responsive to today's life. We accept students for what they are, and what they can do—not for what they wear or with whom they sleep. Least of all do we care about their color or whether they burn incense. We either want them or we don't."

Yale has bent its rigid rules slightly, although not so far as some other schools. There is a tendency to consider civil rights synonymous with the right of blacks. Actually, the admission of an Indian girl to a University of New Mexico sorority—the first in history—was hailed as a landmark by campus leaders. Just as important was a Mexican joining a fraternity on a Texas campus. Moreover, Catholics and Jews now find religion rarely a barrier for fraternity selection, although some student prejudices naturally still exist.

Many local fraternities and sororities are planning more emphasis on service than social activities—responding to campus trends of the day. Some local organizations have undertaken socially oriented projects such as civil rights in housing in surrounding areas. Sororities, particularly on a local level, have found social work more satisfying as a chapter project. The use of projects in welfare and poverty areas has been used as a substitute for hazing by other fraternities and sororities. "Hell" nights have become "Help" nights at some schools. Some fraternities have taken renewed interest in assisting in the mediation of campus issues between faculty and student dissident groups. In fact, it is the failure of the fraternity system to exert leadership in the areas of student concern that has caused much student apathy toward them.

"The 'Greeks' really did nothing to respond to campus student demands," commented a University of Chicago junior. "They were supposed to be campus leaders, but they allowed the militants to take over in creating a new campus-faculty dialogue. If they had been more sensitive to campus demands, they would be much more important today, and rely less on their drinking parties."

On another level, the radical change of living habits and faculties has had its effect on the importance of the fraternity and sorority house. The new-styled dormitories, many of them coed, provide compatible living, and a broad social atmosphere that competes favorably with the best fraternity houses. New dormitories like those at Michigan State provide social programs, libraries, organizations, and even swimming pools. The new buildings such as at New Hampshire University, stratified sex-wise by floors, have changed old-line prisonlike dormitories into socially oriented areas for complete student living. Room dating, now widely available on a broad basis, has affected the role of the fraternity and sorority house. Liberalized off-campus rules permitting students to rent apartments have weakened the fraternity-house appeal. Brightly designed university-built apartments, such as those constructed by the University of Pennsylvania and Florida, make the fraternity and sorority rooms less appealing as residences.

The result is that students still join fraternities and sororities for the purpose of social gatherings and drinking, but without reliance on the eating and residence facilities that so long played an important role in maintaining the fraternity.

One aspect of fraternity and sorority life now coming under fire is the hazing or initiation rite. Hazing goes back to the earliest days of fraternity life. Hazing, it is said, was meant to test the pledge's fortitude and desire to join the group, and his ability to withstand pressure reveal to the nature of the secret rites to others. Long a subject of controversy, it was outlawed for awhile in the twenties when initiation activities caused serious injuries and an occasional fatality.

Since the Korean and Vietnam wars, students have displayed a growing impatience with the initiation procedures.

"They are a lot of damn nonsense," said a Tulane junior. "Looking back, I think we lost some good men because of it."

Many students are not only concerned with the foolishness of hazing, but the extra time involved in the pledging procedures seriously interferes with study time. Students today carry a much heavier load than they did decades ago. And staying in college is frequently a matter of draft exemption.

"I quit pledging when I found I'd probably make the fraternity—and get bounced out for bad marks," said an Oregon sophomore.

There is a growing awareness of the unwillingness of new pledges to accept extensive hazing, especially since so many of the fraternities will have no postgraduate significance, and their roles in schools are lessened. Some West Point cadets, who long cherished the abusing of first-year cadets with a schedule of extended misery, have relented in recent years—a breach of tradition old West Pointers look at with dismay.

In summary, fraternities and sororities are here to stay— fulfilling a need students feel still exists. There is a continuing requirement for the group that enables the individual to "belong"—to identify and to participate—a basic need in the life of most college students. The form of such groups is changing. The socially oriented or superior, autocratic fraternity and sorority with its isolated quarters and quarantined social life is disappearing from the campus. In its place, a more democratic fraternal and sister organization is appearing, which students accept or reject for what it is—a meeting place to provide friends or to pursue special activities. It may be sports—which sustain many fraternities—leisuretime engagements, social work, or just drinking. Many students find similar kinship in other activities or groups. These individuals feel that not joining a fraternity or sorority no longer carries with it a social stigma or feeling of insecurity.

The local fraternity or sorority is growing in importance. The national groups will survive only if they continue to be more responsive to the democratic spirit on the campus. In general, the influence of fraternities and sororities on the campus is on the wane, the College Poll shows. But their usefulness may be increasing.

CHAPTER FIFTEEN

Students Speak off the Record

The basic substance of what college students think or say about topics that truly strike a nerve with them is seldom reported to the press or even relayed to their homes. One of the purposes of the College Poll was to provide a dormitory view of the university campus, to supply a record of student opinions that might serve to bridge the gap between generations. Most of these opinions are expressed to other students—to roommates, to dates, to fraternity brothers, but rarely to parents.

They have interesting attitudes. College Poll interviewers covered sources of questions intended to provide a true consensus of the feelings of our university men and women in the wide and sensitive area of family relationship. In most cases the answers are reassuring if provocative.

For example, much is heard about the so-called generation gap. How bad is the generation gap? Is it really as bad as parents believe?

Students have quite a different view. They were asked the question: "There is much talk about the generation gap. Do you, in fact, disagree with your parents on basic issues and values—and if so, how much?"

Sixty-four percent of all students said they disagree with

their parents only slightly. Twenty-nine percent admitted they disagreed a great deal, and 7 percent said they didn't disagree at all.

"It's not how much you disagree, it's what you disagree about," explained a Santa Clara sophomore. "We disagree about some fundamentals, like honesty and hypocrisy. But they have a different viewpoint—and I guess it's a different era."

"It all hinges on the fact that my parents place more emphasis on materialistic gain than I do," explained a Rutgers junior. "I'd say that sums up most of it."

On the other side of the coin, a Houston junior had this to say: "My parents won't accept any change. And they won't accept any original ideas. Everything is radical to them."

Most students believe the generation gap disagreement stems from three causes: (1) lack of parental willingness to accept change; (2) too much materialism; and (3) unwillingness of parents to discuss issues and ideas with their children.

"Mom and Pop still live in the era of family bossism," said a Boston University senior. "That's an old era—but they are old people."

However, students take a lighter attitude toward parents than people realize. At a twenty-fifth anniversary party given by a Trinity College senior, he proposed this toast to his parents:

"I wish to congratulate my parents on twenty-five years of absolute dictatorship," he said. He brought down the house.

Asked to describe parents as being strict or not strict, 62 percent of those questioned said not strict.

And as an indication, students were asked what type of parents would they be—"strict or not strict?" Sixty-two percent said not strict.

"I don't believe in marrying the girl just like the girl that married dear old Dad," said an Indiana sophomore. "But Mom has done a great job with us kids—even if she was a little square."

"My parents are divorced, but they did the best they could for me, despite a bad marriage," commented a Duke senior.

"I can't communicate too much with my parents," admitted a Gettysburg senior. "But after all, that's not necessary to respect them."

Parents evoke considerable anxiety among students. They worry about their parents' health, and show a deep concern for their fathers' jobs and business success. And this is not occasioned solely by the element of financial security. Most students realize that parents work hard for their children. They also are aware that the world is hard and competitive. Many students "feel sorry" for their fathers.

"He works too hard" was a typical comment. "He never really relaxes."

To parents who look forward to their sons entering the family business, the comment of a Georgetown student is a fair warning.

"My father wants me to go into his automobile business," he stated. "This business has nearly killed him. He's worked for a lifetime at it—six days a week. I hate it not for the money he's made. I hate it for what it has done to him. He'll never know why I don't want to go in with him."

Asked "Do you believe your parents are happy?", 43 percent said yes, 38 percent said no, and 19 percent said they weren't sure or didn't know.

"I guess my parents are happy, but I think it is better to say they are probably not unhappy," said a Florida State coed.

Few students felt their parents were "very happy." But those who did have very happy lives themselves.

"My parents just exist," said a Tufts senior. "They don't seem to have any fun. But I guess they are happy."

"My mother and father seem to get along" was the way a Temple coed explained it. "That's more than a lot of parents do."

To most students the generation gap was never wider than when they were discussing such abstract ideas as "happiness" with their parents.

"If I ever asked my father whether he was happy, he'd think I was nuts," said a Hofstra senior.

"You must never talk about things like that to your father. He wants to believe you are happy and that you feel you are making him happy," said a Smith junior. "Besides, you can tell more from how they act than what they say. I can talk to Mom about things somewhat better."

One way of helping to bridge the generation gap and improving the lack of communication can be found in the matter of letters to students at college. Most students feel they do not get enough mail from home.

"Father never writes, except to send a check," said a Rosemont student. "He's an editor and writes wonderfully, but he rarely writes to me."

"I'd like more news from home—what the kids are doing, what's going on with Mom and Pop," said a Kentucky sophomore. "My folks don't seem to feel that's important."

Students all admit they have been homesick at least once a year. While it's worse around holidays, they get homesick for many reasons and at strange times.

"Every so often I hear a song my mother liked," a Washington and Jefferson student admitted. "I really miss home then."

"I'd like to talk to my father on Sunday mornings like we used to," observed a Minnesota sophomore. "That hits home once in a while."

Are students themselves happy? College Poll studies show that 73 percent of all students felt that they were "basically happy"—happier than their parents were, in fact.

"Of course, I'm happy," replied a typical Ohio State coed. "Things aren't perfect but they never are."

"If we weren't happy, we'd be out of our minds," a Princeton senior declared. "We're a lucky generation."

Coeds are slightly happier than male students, but more coeds are undecided about how they feel than men on the campus.

Interestingly enough, an analysis shows that a college student is more likely to be happy if he (or she):

—comes from a big family
—believes in God or a Supreme Being
—has definite political beliefs
—has parents who are not divorced
—is taking a definite course as opposed to a general course
—lives on campus and has a roommate
—comes from a small town (50,000 population or less)

Most college students talk more about dates than campus riots in their dormitory bull sessions, the College Poll reveals. In fact, student demands on campus issues as a subject is far down the list of collegiate gossip.

Students were asked the question: "What do you talk about on campus—particularly in your room or dormitory bull session?"

Male students placed "dates and dating" first; "teachers and courses," second; "sports," third; "Vietnam and the draft," fourth; and "campus issues," fifth.

Coeds agree that "dates and dating" are first among the girls. They put "teachers and courses" second; "clothes," third; "careers or marriage," fourth; and "campus issues," fifth.

Both coeds and male college students put "politics" sixth, and "parents and home life," seventh.

"You're so fed up with studies and term papers that you look forward to girls and a date," said a Kansas State senior. "Most students have had it with talk about confrontations and campus politics."

"A few students are always crying 'apathy' and want to talk up the problems we have on campus," explained a Columbia sophomore. "But when we're alone in the dorms, the subject generally turns to girls, sex, or problems with a particular teacher or subject."

"During the football season, it's all gung-ho for the team," a Michigan State junior declared. "We all have pigskin fever on the campus. And if it's not for the Spartans, it's for the Detroit Lions. But after football season is over, it's back to dates and the girls, mostly."

A Vietnam veteran who attends Missouri put it another way. "Dormitory talk isn't much different from barracks talk—but cleaner. Most of the guys talk about girls and dates they really never had. They talk about teachers the way we talked about the officers—some good and some bad. There are always a few offbeats who try to raise hell and get everybody stirred up, just like they have in every outfit. In the service, he's in the clink right away. Here he gets his name in the paper."

Coeds have a slightly different outlook. Naturally boys and dates are top priority topics in sorority houses and dormitories. College girls also put school courses and teachers as a top subject. But clothes, fashions, and the like have a high rating in campus conversations.

"It's men, men, and mostly men," said a Radcliffe sophomore. "We've been discussing coed problems with Harvard —but even that really comes down to talking about men."

"Naturally dating is very important in college," said a Miami U. arts major. "Girls always talk about their dates— no details, of course, but the kinds of boys we meet. Part of going to college is learning about men and life—and you learn from the experiences of others as well as yourself."

"We like to talk about clothes and fashions," a Syracuse economics coed replied. "You don't dress up too much at college, but that doesn't mean girls aren't interested in fashions and styles. We always read the Sunday papers and *Vogue* whenever we can get them."

Campus life has changed a great deal from the Roaring Twenties as far as school spirit is concerned. It's true that college enthusiasm runs high in the peak sporting weeks, especially in colleges that have winning football or basketball teams. But the feeling on the campus is that school spirit is at a low ebb. The College Poll asked this question: "How would you rate school spirit at your college?" Only 17 percent of the students said good; whereas 48.6 percent said poor. The balance felt it was only fair.

Astute observers of the college scene have felt that the decline in college spirit is due to professionalism in college sports. Many students agree with this attitude, yet the majority do not feel that the play-for-pay boys have taken over the campus athletic activity. Seven out of ten students stated that there was not too much professionalism in college athletics. However, the reasons are different from what might be implied from the answers.

Intercollegiate sports are declining on many campuses. Football, for example, has become an expensive luxury to many colleges—and each year intercollegiate gridiron competition offers fewer regularly scheduled games. The cost of supporting a college team, with scholarships, a coaching staff, a stadium, and other subsidies is a burden numerous cash-pressed universities have had to forego. In their place schools like Fordham in New York have established "club" football, which is subsidized mostly out of student and alumni funds.

Started a few years ago, the "club" football movement has spread, and returned to the campus much of the student identification with intercollegiate sports that is enjoyed years ago. Now, students can "go out" for football in some colleges and find that the team is not filled by recruited high school stars. The "club" movement has spread to other sports

like rugby, soccer, tennis, and golf, with schools playing informal schedules without varsity recognition or school financial support.

This "club" activity is backed up by an in-depth intramural
program that is largely a schedule of interfraternity sports
competition and, in some cases, an interdormitory schedule
of football, basketball, and baseball. In some schools, the
College Poll figures show, nearly 50 percent of the student
body is engaged in intramural sports programs.

Basketball and touch football are the leading and regular
active college sports, according to the College Poll. Softball,
tennis, and soccer are next. Handball is making a strong
comeback in some areas and in the Northeast, skiing is a
major activity.

The College Poll reveals that the emphasis on college
sports is participation, not spectator activity, and it is this
trend that influences campus opinion to the effect that
actually there is not too much professionalism in sports.

The fact that college athletes make large sums of money
in professional sports after graduation is no of concern to
most college students. An O. J. Simpson and a Joe Namath
are campus heroes during their college days. If they make
good after graduation, students are generally inclined to
applaud their success. Moreover, as an athlete at Ohio State
pointed out to a College Poll interviewer, "Very few college
stars make it in professional sports. Out of thousands who
graduate each year, only a handful make the professional
football draft and even fewer individuals survive the cut.
Most college football and basketball stars end their playing
careers in college. Their real future lies in coaching or physical training teaching."

College athletes, or "jocks," as they are called on campus,
have an isolated existence—out of the mainstream of campus
activity. Their scholarships bind them to rigid practice,
training, and travel schedules, leaving them little time for

other campus activities. They also generally live together, and constitute a small, closely knit group who work hard for their college degrees.

As for student riots and activists, a Louisana State coed freshman, who comes from the East, put it typically: "Well, in every dorm there is usually one girl who feels strongly about civil rights and such topics. Every so often we talk about it. But these conversations usually don't get anywhere. It's like arguing about religion. Most girls have one good argument about it when they first room together—to find out where each stands. Then it only comes up once in a while— even though there's usually someone prodding us to fight."

College Poll surveys have shown that "better teachers and teaching" are a prime student demand. The results of the campus gossip study reveal that this topic is constantly coming up in the off-study hours.

"A teacher can make or break you. And we're always exchanging comments on how good this professor is, how he marks, how much work he demands, and so forth," explained a Cornell sophomore. "Poor teachers are particularly the subject of gossip. Stories pass around pretty fast on the idiosyncrasies and characteristics of each professor. Everyone is interested in that."

"There's a lot of talk about courses and assignments. Believe it or not, homework and classwork are often the big topics on dates. A girl can help you a lot in getting perspective on a particular problem," said a Boston U. sophomore.

In schools where demonstrations have taken place or riots occur, the campus talk about confrontations is higher. Students at colleges like Florida State, Columbia, Stanford, and Berkeley find campus unrest more frequently discussed.

"When police are on the campus, you find it hard to talk about anything else for a while," a Berkeley student told the poll interviewers. "It's a drag after a while."

Students do discuss current events at the time they are

hot news. For example, the *Pueblo* incident was an interesting campus topic during the spring of 1969. Students followed the case with special interest since, in the opinion of many campus pundits, it had overtones of a "navy whitewash."

At the time, College Poll studies showed that few students felt that the *Pueblo* commander was, in fact, a hero. Sixty-five percent of all students answered no to the question: "Was Commander Bucher of the *Pueblo* a naval hero?" Even more at issue was whether or not he performed his duties as a naval officer. Fifty-three percent said he satisfactorily performed his duties as a commanding officer; 15 percent said he didn't, but the remaining students weren't sure.

Students followed Ralph Nader's fight against Detroit with great interest. Most students agreed with Mr. Nader's feeling that cars could be made safer. Sixty-nine percent of all students answered yes to the College Poll question: "Would safer cars, as recommended by Mr. Nader, bring less traffic deaths?"

In addition, campus opinion favors stronger laws regulating drunken driving. It was pointed out that, in many countries, conviction of drunken driving brings a jail sentence. Yet students voted 76 percent in favor of such laws in this country.

Students also discuss drinking and drinking laws a great deal in campus bull sessions.

"Beer is a college man's vitamins," a college dean has said. Many colleges are located in dry states, and in states that have drinking law restrictions for those under twenty-one years of age. Students are incensed at these laws, especially since many come from states that allow eighteen-year-olds drinking privileges. This lack of continuity and coordination with the laws is a constant irritation and cause of frequent brushes with local officials.

Laws like these, where different standards are applied to

the same act, confound students. Eighty percent of all students feel the drinking law for eighteen-year-olds should be standard. Students travel the country more than their parents, and thus see the inequality of laws in operation.

Going to court in Pennsylvania for an offense that doesn't exist in New York—based on the same act—is "hypocrisy" to college students.

Where do students get their information? Most of them listen to the radio regularly. Many campuses have their own radio stations that pipe in news and music. They also carry campus events. Students watch television mostly on weekends, although they monitor key programs like *Rowan and Martin,* and certain specials. *The Eleven O'Clock News* is a popular program on most campuses. Students read newsmagazines like *Newsweek* and *Time* regularly and also photo magazines like *Look* and *Life.* Local newspapers are not too popular with students who live on campus except in large urban areas where the metropolitan newspapers get a big play. Actually, members of the college community obtain their news from a variety of sources and are critical of the coverage of events—a frequent subject for discussion in campus bull sessions.

In conclusion, this college generation appears to be quite like their parents who placed social relationships high on the list of campus conversation. A professor of history at a leading Pennsylvania coed university made this observation:

"These boys and girls don't spend their time plotting and planning the downfall of their university or society. That's the province of a very few. Most of them are serious about their studies and demand more and more of their professors —which is good for all of us. They are smart and well informed. I find they can converse on any subject better than previous generations. But they still act up with the full moon, fall in love, and cheer at football and basketball games as they have over the years. Sometimes I wish they'd let go a little more and have a little more fun. No, I'd say they don't want the end of the university at all. I find them a wonderful group of young men and women. They come at a good time, too. We need an outstanding generation to solve our world problems."

INDEX

Index